Generative AI Demystified

From GPT to Stable Diffusion: Tools to Empower Your Creativity

THOMPSON CARTER

Table of Content

TABLE OF CONTENTS

INTRODUCTION

Welcome to **Generative AI Demystified: From GPT to Stable Diffusion – Tools to Empower Your Creativity**. In a world where **artificial intelligence** is becoming increasingly integral to our lives, this book serves as a comprehensive guide to understanding and harnessing the power of **generative AI** for creative purposes. Whether you're a writer, artist, designer, or technologist, this book is designed to provide you with the knowledge and tools you need to leverage AI in your own creative endeavors.

Generative AI: A Game-Changer for Creativity

Generative AI refers to a class of models capable of **creating new content**—whether it's **text**, **images**, **music**, or even **video**—based on a given input. Unlike traditional AI, which is typically used for tasks like classification and prediction, generative AI goes a step further, allowing machines to produce original works, mimicking human-like creativity. The advent of models like **GPT (Generative Pretrained Transformer)**, **DALL·E**, **Stable Diffusion**, and **GANs (Generative Adversarial Networks)** has opened new frontiers in creativity, enabling anyone with access to these tools to generate high-quality, customized content with just a few clicks or prompts.

While AI has often been seen as a disruptive force, we are now entering a phase where **humans and AI can work together** as collaborators. Generative AI is empowering creators to push the boundaries of their fields, helping to speed up production, inspire new ideas, and even offer fresh perspectives on established creative processes. The true potential of generative AI lies in its ability to **augment human creativity**—not replace it—but to work **alongside artists, writers, designers, and technologists** to bring ideas to life faster and in ways that were once impossible.

The Power of Collaboration: AI as a Creative Partner

Throughout this book, we will explore how generative AI is transforming creative industries such as **art, fashion, music, writing**, and **advertising**. You will learn not just how to use AI, but how to **integrate it into your creative process**. From AI-powered content generation tools that assist with **brainstorming ideas, creating content variations**, and **automating repetitive tasks**, to **cutting-edge models** that generate **new images** or **write compelling narratives** from scratch, the possibilities for AI in creativity are vast.

One of the core themes of this book is **human-AI collaboration**. As we move forward, it's important to recognize that AI is not a replacement for human talent but a powerful tool that can assist in the creative process. Whether you are an artist looking for new ways to express your vision, a writer trying to overcome a block, or a marketer in need of personalized content at scale, AI can serve as a co-creator, offering suggestions, generating variations, and enhancing your ideas with new possibilities.

Understanding the Foundations of Generative AI

For those new to the world of AI, this book will also provide you with a solid understanding of the underlying concepts of generative AI. We'll introduce key principles like **machine learning, neural networks**, and **deep learning**, and show you how they enable the creation of generative models. We will explore a range of tools and frameworks, including **TensorFlow, PyTorch**, and **HuggingFace**, providing you with the foundation to not only use existing models but also **build your own**. Whether you're a beginner with no prior AI experience or an expert looking to refine your knowledge, this book will help you unlock the power of AI in a way that is **accessible** and **actionable**.

Real-World Examples and Case Studies

One of the best ways to understand the impact of generative AI is through **real-world applications**. In this book, we will showcase how industry leaders, artists, designers, writers, and musicians are already using AI to create remarkable works. For example, you'll discover how **AI-generated art** is being used in galleries, **AI-driven fashion** is transforming the way clothes are designed, and **AI-generated music** is changing the way we compose and experience sound. These examples will demonstrate not just the power of

AI but its **limitless potential** when combined with human creativity.

Through these case studies, we will also examine how AI is being used to tackle the most challenging creative problems—from **scaling content creation** in advertising to **enhancing storytelling** in video games. You'll gain a deeper appreciation for the **collaborative nature** of AI and creativity and be inspired to incorporate these tools into your own work.

A Vision for the Future

The future of generative AI is bright and full of possibilities. As the technology continues to evolve, we are bound to see even more **innovative** and **exciting** applications across all fields of creativity. But with great power comes great responsibility. In the final chapters of this book, we will also look at the **ethical implications** of generative AI, addressing concerns around **bias**, **data privacy**, and **misuse**. We'll discuss how to approach AI as a **creative tool** while being mindful of its societal impact, and how we can ensure that these technologies are developed and used responsibly.

What You Will Learn in This Book

In this book, you will learn:

- **How generative AI works**, from the foundational concepts to advanced techniques.
- **How to use AI tools** like **GPT, Stable Diffusion**, and **GANs** for your creative projects.
- **The ethics of AI** in creative industries and how to use AI responsibly.
- **Practical steps** to integrate AI into your workflow, whether you're in art, music, fashion, writing, or another field.
- **Real-world examples** of how AI is changing creative industries and how you can apply AI to your own work.

This book is designed to be both **practical and inspiring**, giving you the tools and understanding to start using generative AI immediately while providing you with a broader vision of the future possibilities that AI brings to the creative process.

As we embark on this journey into the world of generative AI, let's embrace the possibilities it offers. AI is no longer a far-off futuristic concept—it's here, it's accessible, and it's ready to help you create like never before.

Let's dive in and explore the **endless potential of generative AI** in creativity!

CHAPTER ONE

Introduction to Generative AI

What is Generative AI?

Generative AI refers to a class of artificial intelligence models designed to create new data that resembles existing data. Unlike traditional AI models, which are focused on recognizing patterns and making predictions from data, **generative models** are capable of generating entirely new content. This can include anything from text, images, and audio to videos, and even entire 3D environments.

Generative AI is built on complex neural networks, particularly **deep learning** architectures, that are trained to understand the underlying structure and patterns within a dataset. Once trained, these models can generate novel outputs that maintain the same statistical properties as the original data.

For example:

- A **text generation** model (like GPT-3) can write essays, poems, or even code based on a prompt.
- An **image generation** model (like Stable Diffusion) can create realistic artwork or design concepts from text descriptions.

What makes generative AI unique is its ability to "create" rather than simply "classify" or "predict," opening up an entire spectrum of applications, particularly in **creativity** and **artificial content generation**.

History and Evolution of AI Technologies

To fully appreciate the significance of generative AI, it's important to understand the broader context of **artificial intelligence (AI)** and how it has evolved over the years:

1. **Early AI (1950s-1970s)**:
    o AI started as a field focused on logical reasoning and rule-based systems. The earliest AI models were designed to mimic human decision-making but were limited to well-defined, rule-based tasks.
    o **Alan Turing** introduced the **Turing Test** in 1950, proposing that a machine could be considered intelligent if it could engage in a conversation indistinguishable from a human.
2. **Symbolic AI (1980s-1990s)**:
    o During this period, researchers focused on building expert systems, which used knowledge representation and logical rules to simulate human expertise in specific domains (e.g., medical diagnosis, legal reasoning).

o These systems were highly specialized but lacked the ability to handle real-world variability and uncertainty.

3. **Rise of Machine Learning (2000s-Present)**:
   o The turn of the 21st century brought about a shift toward **machine learning (ML)**, where models could learn patterns from large datasets without explicit programming. This laid the foundation for the development of **supervised learning** and **unsupervised learning**.
   o **Deep learning**—a subset of machine learning—emerged in the late 2000s and 2010s, using neural networks with many layers (hence "deep") to automatically extract features and learn patterns from raw data. This led to breakthroughs in fields such as **speech recognition**, **computer vision**, and **natural language processing (NLP)**.

4. **Generative AI (2010s-Present)**:
   o Generative AI emerged as a natural extension of deep learning, with models capable of creating novel content. The advent of **Generative Adversarial Networks (GANs)**, introduced by **Ian Goodfellow** in 2014, was a major milestone in generative modeling. GANs allowed for the generation of realistic images by pitting two neural networks (the generator and the discriminator) against each other.

- o **Variational Autoencoders (VAEs)** and other architectures followed, enabling generative models to produce images, text, and even music.
- o In recent years, **transformers** have revolutionized NLP, with models like **GPT-3** taking text generation to new heights. **Stable Diffusion, DALL·E**, and **MidJourney** are some of the most notable advancements in generative image models.

Generative AI, as we know it today, is the product of years of research and development across multiple domains of AI, combining powerful models with large datasets and immense computational resources. Its evolution has opened up new possibilities in both creative and practical domains.

How Generative AI is Revolutionizing Creativity

Generative AI is having a profound impact on creativity, providing tools that enhance and democratize creative work. Here's how generative AI is revolutionizing creativity:

1. **Art and Design**:
   - o AI-powered tools like **Stable Diffusion**, **DALL·E**, and **MidJourney** allow artists and designers to generate unique visual art, illustrations, and concept designs

from simple text prompts. These tools are not just for generating art in a traditional sense but also for exploring new creative avenues by offering a wide range of styles, themes, and visualizations that might not have been previously considered.

o Generative models can create highly detailed images that can serve as inspiration or be used directly in projects, significantly accelerating the design process.

2. **Writing and Content Creation**:

o **Text generation models** like **GPT-3** have taken writing to new heights, enabling the generation of essays, blogs, poetry, stories, and even code. For writers, these models act as assistants that help with brainstorming, structuring content, and even improving grammar and style.

o Beyond just content generation, these models can personalize content creation at scale. For example, AI can tailor marketing copy to specific audiences or write personalized emails and letters.

3. **Music and Audio**:

o **AI-powered music generation** tools like **OpenAI's MuseNet** and **Amper Music** allow users to generate original music tracks in a variety of genres, with minimal input. These tools can assist musicians in creating new compositions, experimenting with different sounds, or even creating background music for films and videos.

o In audio production, generative models are used to enhance voice recordings, generate new sound effects, and even mimic specific voices, opening up new possibilities for content creators in media production.

4. **Video and Animation**:

o The generation of realistic or stylized video content is another exciting frontier in creative AI. Models that generate video from text descriptions (text-to-video) are in early development, but already, tools like **RunwayML** allow creators to generate deepfake videos, animate still images, or create dynamic content with minimal effort.

o In the gaming industry, AI is used to generate vast, procedurally-created environments, characters, and narratives, leading to more immersive and dynamic experiences for players.

5. **Interactive Creativity**:

o Generative AI is enabling **collaborative creativity**, where humans and machines work together in a symbiotic relationship. Rather than AI replacing human artists, musicians, and writers, it serves as a tool that enhances the creative process. For example, AI might generate multiple options for a design, but the artist makes the final decision, combining human judgment with machine creativity.

Real-World Examples: How Companies are Using Generative AI Today

Generative AI is already making an impact across various industries. Here are some real-world examples of companies and sectors using generative AI to innovate:

1. **OpenAI**:
   o OpenAI's **GPT-3** has transformed the content creation industry. Companies like **Copy.ai** and **Jasper.ai** use GPT-3 to automate copywriting, creating marketing materials, blog posts, and social media content with minimal human input.
   o OpenAI's **DALL·E** and **CLIP** are changing the way designers and marketers generate visual content. Companies use these tools to create custom graphics and advertisements in seconds.
2. **Adobe**:
   o Adobe's **Adobe Sensei** uses generative AI to automate tasks in design and video editing. It helps users by suggesting edits, creating patterns, and even generating new elements for design projects based on existing data.

- Adobe is also integrating AI tools like **Photoshop's Neural Filters,** which allow users to modify portraits and photos with the help of deep learning algorithms.

3. **DeepMind**:
   - DeepMind, known for its advances in reinforcement learning and deep learning, has also contributed to generative models in various fields. For example, **AlphaFold**, a system that generates accurate 3D models of proteins, has revolutionized the field of biology by aiding in drug discovery and genetic research.

4. **NVIDIA**:
   - **NVIDIA** has leveraged generative AI for creating photorealistic 3D environments and characters, particularly in gaming and entertainment. Their **GANverse3D** tool generates 3D models from a single 2D image, simplifying the 3D modeling process in game development and animation.

5. **Content Creation Startups**:
   - Startups like **Artbreeder** and **Runway ML** have democratized the use of generative models for artists and creators. Artbreeder allows users to create unique artworks by blending and evolving images using AI, while Runway ML offers an easy-to-use platform for generating AI-driven visuals, videos, and even text.

Summary

Generative AI is not just a buzzword—it is transforming creativity across multiple domains, offering new ways for people to create, explore, and innovate. By understanding the fundamentals of generative models, their evolution, and the impact they're having today, we gain insight into the future of AI-powered creativity. From **GPT-3** and **Stable Diffusion** to the applications in music, design, and video production, generative AI is enabling us to push the boundaries of what's possible.

In the next chapters, we'll dive deeper into the **specific techniques** and **tools** behind generative AI, explore hands-on examples, and discuss how you can leverage these technologies in your own creative endeavors. Whether you're an artist, writer, designer, or developer, generative AI offers powerful tools to enhance your work and expand your creative horizons.

CHAPTER TWO

Understanding Artificial Intelligence and Machine Learning

Basic Concepts of AI and Machine Learning

Artificial Intelligence (AI) and Machine Learning (ML) are two interconnected fields, but they have distinct differences. Let's break down the basic concepts to build a strong foundation for understanding how these technologies work and how they relate to Generative AI.

Artificial Intelligence (AI) refers to the broader concept of machines or computers performing tasks that would typically require human intelligence. These tasks can include reasoning, problem-solving, understanding language, learning, and perception. AI aims to create machines that can mimic human cognitive functions and decision-making processes.

On the other hand, **Machine Learning (ML)** is a subset of AI. ML focuses on creating algorithms and models that allow computers to learn from data without being explicitly programmed for each task. Instead of providing a computer with a fixed set of rules, we expose it to large datasets, allowing the model to infer patterns and make predictions based on that data. Essentially, ML enables a system to "learn" from past experiences and improve over time.

There are different types of machine learning, each designed to tackle different kinds of problems. But before diving into those specifics, it's important to understand the fundamental idea behind machine learning: **training a model**.

When we train a machine learning model, we provide it with input data (features) and corresponding output (labels or target values). Over time, the model learns to predict the output from the input data by adjusting its parameters. This is how **training** works—by optimizing the model to make better predictions.

Supervised, Unsupervised, and Reinforcement Learning

There are three primary categories of machine learning based on how the model is trained: **supervised learning**, **unsupervised learning**, and **reinforcement learning**. Each of these categories has unique characteristics and applications.

1. **Supervised Learning**:
    - **Definition**: In supervised learning, the model is trained on a labeled dataset. This means that for each input data point, the correct output is already provided (i.e., the "labels"). The model learns to map the inputs to the correct outputs, and its performance is evaluated based on how well it predicts these labels.

- o **Goal**: The goal of supervised learning is to make predictions or classifications based on input data.
- o **Examples**:
  - **Classification**: Predicting whether an email is spam or not (binary classification) or identifying the species of an animal based on its features (multi-class classification).
  - **Regression**: Predicting the price of a house based on its features (e.g., size, location, number of rooms).
- o **Real-World Example**: Training a **facial recognition system** to identify faces in images. The training data consists of images (input) labeled with the identity of the people in those images (output).

2. **Unsupervised Learning**:
   - o **Definition**: In unsupervised learning, the model is trained on data that is not labeled. The goal is for the model to learn the underlying structure or patterns in the data without having predefined categories or labels.
   - o **Goal**: The goal is to discover hidden patterns, groupings, or associations within the data.
   - o **Examples**:
     - **Clustering**: Grouping similar customers based on purchasing

behavior (e.g., market segmentation).

- **Dimensionality Reduction**: Reducing the number of features in a dataset while preserving important information (e.g., Principal Component Analysis, or PCA).

o **Real-World Example: Customer segmentation** for marketing. A company uses unsupervised learning to segment its customers into distinct groups based on purchasing behavior, allowing for more targeted marketing strategies.

3. **Reinforcement Learning**:

o **Definition**: In reinforcement learning, the model learns by interacting with an environment and receiving feedback in the form of rewards or penalties. The model does not receive explicit input-output pairs but instead learns from actions it takes in a given environment.

o **Goal**: The goal is to learn a sequence of actions that maximize a cumulative reward. The model makes decisions based on trial and error, continuously improving its strategy based on the feedback it receives.

o **Examples**:

- **Robotics**: A robot learning to navigate a maze or pick up objects by receiving positive feedback for successful actions.

- **Game-playing AI**: AI models that play games (e.g., chess, Go, or video games), learning to make optimal moves by receiving rewards for winning and penalties for losing.
  - **Real-World Example**: **Self-driving cars** use reinforcement learning to learn how to drive by interacting with their environment. The car makes decisions, such as when to stop or turn, based on feedback in the form of rewards (safe navigation) and penalties (collisions, traffic violations).

How Machine Learning Models Work

To understand how machine learning models function, let's break down the process of building and deploying an ML model:

1. **Data Collection and Preparation**:
   - The first step in any machine learning project is gathering the data. In supervised learning, this means collecting both the features (input data) and labels (target data). In unsupervised learning, we collect only the features.
   - After gathering data, it must be cleaned and preprocessed. This may involve handling missing values, normalizing or scaling data, converting categorical data

into numerical formats, or removing irrelevant features.

2. **Model Selection**:
   - Next, we choose the type of machine learning model. The choice depends on the problem at hand (e.g., classification, regression, clustering) and the available data. For instance, decision trees, support vector machines (SVMs), and neural networks are commonly used models.
   - More complex tasks, such as image recognition or natural language processing (NLP), require more sophisticated models, like **Convolutional Neural Networks (CNNs)** or **Recurrent Neural Networks (RNNs)**.

3. **Training the Model**:
   - The training process involves feeding the model with input data and labels (in supervised learning) and adjusting its parameters to minimize error. This is typically done by an optimization process like **gradient descent**, where the model iteratively adjusts to find the optimal parameters.
   - During training, the model learns patterns in the data and fine-tunes its parameters to improve prediction accuracy.

4. **Evaluation**:
   - After training, we evaluate the model's performance on a separate test dataset (which was not used during training) to

assess how well the model generalizes to unseen data.
- Common evaluation metrics include accuracy, precision, recall, F1-score (for classification), and mean squared error (for regression).

5. **Model Deployment**:
   - Once the model performs well on test data, it can be deployed into a real-world environment, where it will make predictions on new, unseen data. This step may involve integrating the model into a larger software system or application.

Real-World Example: From Image Classification to Self-Driving Cars

To bring all these concepts together, let's explore two real-world applications of machine learning:

1. **Image Classification**:
   - Imagine a company that wants to develop an AI system to automatically classify medical images as either benign or malignant. This task involves **supervised learning**, where the model is trained on a dataset of labeled images (e.g., X-rays or MRIs) along with their corresponding labels (benign or malignant).
   - The model learns to extract features from the images, such as shapes, textures, or patterns, and uses these features to

classify new, unseen images. **Convolutional Neural Networks (CNNs)** are particularly well-suited for this task, as they excel at learning spatial hierarchies in image data.

2. **Self-Driving Cars**:
   o Self-driving cars represent a complex problem that involves **reinforcement learning**, as the car needs to interact with its environment and make decisions based on rewards and penalties.
   o For example, a self-driving car learns how to navigate roads by receiving positive feedback for actions like stopping at traffic lights or making safe turns and penalties for things like speeding or causing accidents. The car's AI learns the best sequence of actions to maximize its cumulative reward (safe driving).
   o In addition to reinforcement learning, **computer vision** models are used to help the car recognize objects in its environment (such as pedestrians, other cars, and traffic signs) and make decisions accordingly.

Summary

In this chapter, we laid the groundwork for understanding **Artificial Intelligence (AI)** and **Machine Learning (ML)**. We explored the basic concepts of these technologies and how they enable machines to learn from data, make predictions, and perform complex tasks. We covered the three primary types of machine learning—**supervised learning, unsupervised learning**, and **reinforcement learning**—and looked at how these techniques are applied to real-world scenarios such as **image classification** and **self-driving cars**.

In the next chapters, we will delve deeper into **Generative AI** and how these techniques are harnessed to create new and innovative content. Stay tuned as we move from the foundations to cutting-edge applications in the world of creativity and artificial intelligence.

CHAPTER THREE

The Rise of Generative Models

Introduction to Generative Models

Generative models represent a powerful class of machine learning models that are capable of creating new data. Unlike traditional discriminative models that classify or predict based on existing data (e.g., predicting whether an email is spam or not), generative models take a step further by generating completely new content that resembles the data they have been trained on. These models are designed to capture the underlying distribution of data, enabling them to generate outputs similar to the data they've learned from, but never seen before.

Generative models are a crucial component of **Generative AI**, which has gained significant attention for its ability to create realistic images, videos, text, and even music. The key feature of generative models is their ability to generate entirely new instances of data, as opposed to simply classifying or predicting labels for given data points.

For example, a generative model trained on thousands of paintings can generate new, never-before-seen artwork that still adheres to the artistic styles in the training data. Similarly, a generative text model like **GPT** can write unique essays, stories, or articles, maintaining coherence and style based on the context it has learned.

Generative models are especially important in creative fields such as art, design, and media production. They are also used in more practical applications like drug discovery, data augmentation, and even generating synthetic data for training other models.

Key Concepts: Latent Spaces, Noise, and Sampling

To fully understand how generative models work, we must first explore some foundational concepts that drive their functioning:

1. **Latent Spaces**:
   o **Latent space** refers to the abstract space in which data points are represented in a compressed form. In generative models, this space is often lower-dimensional and captures the essential features or patterns of the data. For example, in an image generation model, a latent space might represent various characteristics of an image (e.g., colors, shapes, textures) in a compressed form.
   o A well-structured latent space enables the model to generate realistic data by sampling points from it. By manipulating or sampling from the latent space, generative models can create diverse

outputs that still adhere to the patterns learned from the training data.

2. **Noise**:
   - Noise is a random input that is typically used to generate new data in generative models. In models like **Generative Adversarial Networks (GANs)** and **Diffusion Models**, noise is fed into the model to produce varied outputs.
   - In GANs, for instance, the generator takes a random noise vector from the latent space and transforms it into an image that looks like something from the training data. The randomness in the noise ensures that the model generates diverse outputs rather than just reproducing the training data.

3. **Sampling**:
   - **Sampling** refers to the process of selecting a point from the latent space or noise distribution in order to generate new data. In generative models, you sample from this space to create diverse and novel instances of data.
   - The quality of the samples depends on the model's training. Well-trained models will produce outputs that closely resemble real data, while poorly trained models might produce unrealistic or distorted outputs.

Popular Generative Models: GANs, VAEs, and Diffusion Models

Several types of generative models have emerged over the years, each with unique characteristics and applications. Let's look at three of the most popular ones:

1. **Generative Adversarial Networks (GANs)**:
    o **GANs**, introduced by **Ian Goodfellow** in 2014, are a class of generative models that use a unique approach called the **adversarial** process. GANs consist of two neural networks:
        ▪ **Generator**: The generator creates new data instances (e.g., images, text, or audio).
        ▪ **Discriminator**: The discriminator evaluates how real or fake the generated data is.
    o The generator and discriminator are trained together in a **zero-sum game**: the generator aims to create data that the discriminator cannot distinguish from real data, while the discriminator strives to correctly classify real and fake data.
    o Over time, the generator gets better at producing realistic data, and the discriminator becomes better at identifying fake data. This adversarial process leads to the generation of highly realistic data, such as images, that can be

used in creative applications or for data augmentation.

Real-World Example: GANs are widely used in the art world to generate **realistic paintings** and artwork. For instance, the **ArtGAN** project uses GANs to generate new art in the style of famous artists, creating novel and unique pieces that resemble works from the classical or modern art world.

2. **Variational Autoencoders (VAEs)**:
   o **VAEs** are another type of generative model, particularly effective for generating data in complex, high-dimensional spaces, such as images or natural language.
   o A VAE consists of two main parts:
     ▪ **Encoder**: The encoder compresses input data (such as an image) into a compact, lower-dimensional **latent space**.
     ▪ **Decoder**: The decoder reconstructs data from the latent space, generating new instances.
   o Unlike GANs, which rely on an adversarial training process, VAEs use a probabilistic approach. They assume that data is generated from a latent distribution and aim to maximize the likelihood of the data given the latent variables.

- VAEs are particularly useful for tasks like **data compression**, **image generation**, and **anomaly detection**.

Real-World Example: VAEs are often used in medical imaging to generate **synthetic medical images** for training other models or improving diagnostic processes. For example, a VAE trained on MRI scans can generate realistic synthetic MRI images for training healthcare AI models.

3. **Diffusion Models**:
   - **Diffusion models** have emerged as one of the most powerful generative models in recent years, particularly for generating high-quality images. These models are based on a process that simulates how data is "destroyed" and then "restored."
   - The process begins with adding noise to an image (or data), and over many iterations, the model learns to reverse this process, gradually reconstructing the original data from noise. This allows diffusion models to generate very high-quality, realistic outputs.
   - Unlike GANs, which train two models (generator and discriminator), diffusion models use a single network and focus on denoising.
   - Diffusion models are notable for their ability to generate diverse outputs without the issues of mode collapse (a problem in

GANs where the generator produces limited variations).

Real-World Example: **Stable Diffusion**, a widely used model, is capable of generating high-quality images based on text prompts, offering a breakthrough in text-to-image generation. This model is used in industries such as design, advertising, and gaming, enabling professionals to rapidly create stunning visuals and concept art.

Real-World Example: Image Generation with GANs

To bring the concepts to life, let's dive into a real-world example of how **Generative Adversarial Networks (GANs)** can be used for **image generation**.

Imagine a fashion company that wants to generate new clothing designs using AI. Instead of manually designing each new piece, the company can train a **GAN** on a dataset of thousands of clothing images. Here's how the process would work:

1. **Data Collection**: The company gathers a dataset of images of various clothing styles, including dresses, jackets, pants, shoes, etc.
2. **Training the GAN**: The GAN is trained with the clothing images, where the **generator** learns to create new clothing designs, and the

discriminator learns to distinguish between real and fake designs.

3. **Generation**: After sufficient training, the generator begins producing new clothing designs that closely resemble the real designs in the dataset. These designs can be highly diverse, showcasing new patterns, colors, and styles that the company can then use as inspiration for future collections.

4. **Quality Control**: The generated designs are reviewed by human designers, who may choose to tweak or refine the generated content. The GAN's ability to produce multiple variations of a design allows the designers to explore creative ideas they might not have considered.

The resulting designs are not limited to the training data but are instead **novel creations** that remain faithful to the style and structure of the original images. In this way, GANs can dramatically enhance the creativity and productivity of designers, while also reducing the time and cost of generating new designs.

Summary

In this chapter, we introduced **Generative AI** and explored the key concepts behind **generative models**. We discussed the role of **latent spaces**, **noise**, and **sampling** in generating new data, and examined popular generative models like **GANs**, **VAEs**, and **diffusion models**. These models have opened up exciting possibilities in creativity and innovation, from generating realistic images and art to assisting in drug discovery and data augmentation.

We also looked at a **real-world example** of using **GANs** for image generation in the fashion industry, illustrating the practical applications of generative models in creative industries.

As we continue to explore the fascinating world of **Generative AI**, we'll dive deeper into more advanced topics and practical implementations, equipping you with the knowledge and tools to use these technologies in your own projects.

CHAPTER FOUR

The Transformer Revolution

What Are Transformers and Why Are They Important?

In the world of artificial intelligence and machine learning, **Transformers** have revolutionized the way models process and understand data, particularly in **Natural Language Processing (NLP)**. Introduced in the 2017 paper **"Attention is All You Need"** by Vaswani et al., the Transformer model has since become the foundation for almost all modern state-of-the-art NLP models, including **GPT-3**, **BERT**, **T5**, and more.

Transformers are a type of **deep learning architecture** that can process sequences of data (such as text, speech, or time-series) in parallel, rather than sequentially like older models such as **Recurrent Neural Networks (RNNs)** or **Long Short-Term Memory networks (LSTMs)**. This parallelism allows Transformers to handle long-range dependencies in data much more efficiently, making them highly scalable and faster to train.

Why are Transformers important?

1. **Parallelization**: Unlike RNNs or LSTMs, which process sequences step-by-step, Transformers allow for the entire sequence to be processed at

once. This significantly speeds up training and allows for better scalability on large datasets.

2. **Handling Long-Range Dependencies**: Traditional models like RNNs struggle with long-term dependencies (e.g., understanding context across long paragraphs of text). Transformers, with their **attention mechanism**, excel in capturing dependencies over long sequences, making them ideal for tasks like language translation, document summarization, and question answering.

3. **Flexibility**: Transformers have proven to be incredibly versatile, not just for NLP tasks but for **vision**, **audio processing**, and even **reinforcement learning**, demonstrating their widespread applicability.

Since their introduction, Transformers have consistently outperformed previous models across a wide range of NLP tasks, from machine translation to text generation and summarization, cementing their place as one of the most influential breakthroughs in AI.

Key Components: Attention Mechanism and Self-Attention

Two key components of the Transformer architecture are **attention** and **self-attention**. Understanding these mechanisms is essential to grasp how Transformers operate and why they are so effective.

1. **Attention Mechanism**:
   - The **attention mechanism** enables the model to focus on different parts of the input data when processing it. In the case of text, the model can "attend" to specific words or phrases that are more relevant for understanding the context or meaning of a sentence.
   - Traditional sequence models like RNNs process input one element at a time, which can limit their ability to capture long-range dependencies. In contrast, **attention** allows the model to directly access any part of the sequence, no matter how far apart the elements are.
   - This flexibility enables Transformers to model complex relationships between different parts of the sequence, making them more effective for tasks like language translation, where understanding relationships between distant words is key.

2. **Self-Attention**:
   - **Self-attention** is a specific form of attention where the model attends to different words in the same sequence. For example, in the sentence "The cat sat on the mat," self-attention would allow the model to understand that "cat" is related to "sat" and that "mat" is the object that the cat sat on.
   - Self-attention computes a set of **attention scores** for each word, showing how much

focus each word should receive in relation to other words in the sequence. These scores help the model weigh the importance of different words when making predictions.

o Self-attention is powerful because it enables the model to capture relationships between words regardless of their position in the sequence. This is particularly useful for tasks like understanding the meaning of long sentences or paragraphs where word order and context matter.

The Impact of Transformers on NLP and Beyond

The introduction of Transformers marked a significant shift in the field of Natural Language Processing (NLP). Before Transformers, models like **RNNs** and **LSTMs** were the standard for sequence processing tasks. However, these models had limitations, such as the inability to process long-range dependencies efficiently and the sequential nature of their computations, which made them slow to train.

With the advent of Transformers, NLP saw a massive leap in performance across a variety of tasks. Let's break down some of the key impacts Transformers have had:

1. **Machine Translation**:

- o Prior to Transformers, machine translation relied on models like **Sequence-to-Sequence (Seq2Seq)** with attention mechanisms, which still had trouble handling long sentences and maintaining context. Transformers, however, excelled in machine translation by leveraging self-attention to better capture long-range dependencies.
- o Models like **Google Translate**, powered by Transformer-based architectures, have dramatically improved in translation quality, enabling more fluent and accurate translations across languages.

2. **Text Generation and Summarization**:
- o **Text generation** has been revolutionized by Transformer-based models. GPT-3, for instance, is capable of generating human-like text based on a prompt, making it useful for tasks ranging from **chatbots** and **customer support** to **creative writing** and **content generation**.
- o **Text summarization** has also benefitted from Transformers, with models being able to generate coherent, concise summaries of long documents while preserving the meaning.

3. **Question Answering and Conversational AI**:
- o Transformers have enabled significant improvements in **question answering** systems, where models can read passages and answer questions based on that text.

For instance, **BERT** (Bidirectional Encoder Representations from Transformers) was designed to understand context by considering words both to the left and right of a target word, making it more effective at answering questions than prior models.

- o **Conversational AI** systems, including **virtual assistants** like Siri and Alexa, have become more accurate and fluent by incorporating Transformer models that better understand and generate natural language.

4. **Beyond NLP: Transformers in Other Domains**:

- o While Transformers initially gained popularity for NLP tasks, their application has expanded to other areas such as **computer vision** (e.g., Vision Transformers), **audio processing**, and even **reinforcement learning**.
- o For instance, **ViT (Vision Transformer)** demonstrated that Transformer-based architectures could perform well on image classification tasks, traditionally dominated by **Convolutional Neural Networks (CNNs)**.

Real-World Example: How GPT-3 Transformed Text Generation

GPT-3 (Generative Pretrained Transformer 3), developed by **OpenAI**, is one of the most well-known examples of a Transformer model. It has shown unprecedented capabilities in natural language understanding and generation, with over 175 billion parameters.

Here's how GPT-3 has transformed text generation and why it's so powerful:

1. **Large-Scale Language Understanding**:
   o GPT-3 is pre-trained on an enormous corpus of text data from diverse sources, which gives it a broad understanding of language. This pre-training allows GPT-3 to generate text that is not only coherent but contextually relevant, making it applicable to a wide range of tasks, such as summarization, translation, and even creative writing.
2. **Zero-Shot and Few-Shot Learning**:
   o One of the most revolutionary aspects of GPT-3 is its ability to perform **zero-shot learning**—it can generate text or perform tasks without being explicitly trained for those tasks. For example, GPT-3 can answer questions, write essays, or create poetry based on a simple prompt.
   o It also performs well in **few-shot learning**, where it can adapt to new tasks

with only a few examples provided. This flexibility has enabled it to be used for a wide variety of applications, such as generating legal documents, customer support responses, or even code.

3. **Creative Content Generation**:
   o GPT-3 has found a place in creative fields like **writing**, where it assists writers by generating ideas, suggesting sentence structures, or even writing entire articles or stories. Many content creators and marketers have adopted GPT-3 to automate writing tasks, saving time and improving efficiency.
   o The model has also been used to generate **poetry** and **dialogue for video games**, showcasing its ability to produce creative, human-like text.

4. **Real-World Applications**:
   o GPT-3 has been integrated into **chatbots**, where it is used to create more natural and human-like conversations. Businesses use GPT-3-based chatbots for customer service, providing quick and accurate responses to customer inquiries.
   o In the **education** sector, GPT-3 is used to create personalized learning materials, quizzes, and even tutoring sessions, helping students learn at their own pace.

Summary

In this chapter, we explored the **Transformer model**, which has transformed the way we approach sequence processing tasks, particularly in **Natural Language Processing (NLP)**. Key components like **attention** and **self-attention** have enabled Transformers to capture long-range dependencies and process data in parallel, leading to better performance across tasks like **text generation, machine translation,** and **question answering**.

We also discussed the **impact of Transformers** on NLP and beyond, particularly how models like **GPT-3** have revolutionized text generation, making it possible to automate tasks that once required human creativity and expertise. From conversational AI to content generation, GPT-3 and other Transformer-based models are pushing the boundaries of what machines can do in language-related tasks.

As we move forward, we will delve into how these powerful models are applied in **Generative AI**, enabling the creation of art, music, and beyond. Stay tuned for a deeper exploration of how you can leverage Transformer-based models for your own creative endeavors.

CHAPTER FIVE

Exploring GPT Models: From GPT-1 to GPT-4

The Evolution of GPT Models

The **GPT (Generative Pretrained Transformer)** series has dramatically changed the landscape of Natural Language Processing (NLP) and has been at the forefront of AI-driven content generation. Starting from GPT-1 in 2018, the GPT models have continuously evolved, increasing in size, capability, and impact. Let's take a look at how the GPT models have evolved over time:

1. **GPT-1 (2018)**:
    o The first version of GPT introduced the concept of **pretraining** and **fine-tuning** in the context of transformer-based models. GPT-1 was a relatively small model, with 117 million parameters, but it demonstrated the potential of transformers for language modeling tasks.
    o **Pretraining** involved training the model on a massive corpus of text data to learn language patterns and structure, while **fine-tuning** allowed the model to be adapted to specific tasks like text classification or question answering.
    o GPT-1 demonstrated that a single transformer model could handle multiple

NLP tasks without task-specific architectures, paving the way for future advancements.

2. **GPT-2 (2019)**:
   o GPT-2 marked a significant improvement over GPT-1 in terms of size and performance. With 1.5 billion parameters, it was much larger and capable of generating more coherent and contextually relevant text.
   o GPT-2 gained widespread attention due to its ability to generate highly realistic text based on a given prompt. It was able to write paragraphs, essays, and even entire articles that were almost indistinguishable from human-written content.
   o However, OpenAI initially hesitated to release the full GPT-2 model due to concerns about its potential misuse in generating fake news, spam, and other harmful content. Eventually, the model was made available, demonstrating its impressive ability to generate human-like text.

3. **GPT-3 (2020)**:
   o With 175 billion parameters, GPT-3 is a massive leap forward from GPT-2. It is one of the largest and most powerful language models to date, and its performance in various NLP tasks is remarkable.
   o GPT-3's ability to generate human-like text and understand complex language

prompts is due to its sheer size and the vast amount of data it was trained on. Unlike its predecessors, GPT-3 is capable of performing tasks with little to no fine-tuning. It can complete a wide range of tasks, from answering questions to writing poetry, with minimal task-specific training.

o GPT-3's **few-shot learning** capability allows it to understand and perform tasks after seeing only a few examples. In many cases, it can perform well with just a simple prompt, making it incredibly versatile and powerful.

4. **GPT-4 (2023)**:

o GPT-4 builds on the success of GPT-3 with even more advanced capabilities, boasting **multimodal** abilities (i.e., processing both text and images) and significantly improving the quality of text generation.

o GPT-4 is designed to be more reliable, creative, and capable of handling nuanced instructions. It also performs better on a wide variety of benchmarks, including tasks requiring reasoning, logic, and common-sense knowledge.

o The size of GPT-4 is not officially disclosed, but it is speculated to have **hundreds of billions** of parameters, allowing it to generate highly sophisticated text, perform complex reasoning, and understand subtle contextual cues better than its predecessors.

- o GPT-4 has also demonstrated a marked improvement in **fact-checking** and the ability to avoid harmful outputs, making it more ethical and reliable for real-world applications.

GPT's Architecture and Mechanism

GPT models are based on the **Transformer architecture**, which uses a mechanism called **self-attention** to process and generate language. Let's break down the key components that make up GPT's architecture and mechanism:

1. **Transformer Architecture**:
   - o At the core of GPT is the **Transformer architecture**, which relies on **self-attention** to process input data (in this case, text) efficiently. The self-attention mechanism allows GPT to focus on different words in a sentence, regardless of their position, and understand the relationships between them.
   - o Unlike Recurrent Neural Networks (RNNs) and Long Short-Term Memory networks (LSTMs), which process text one word at a time in sequence, Transformers can process entire sentences in parallel, making them much

more efficient for large-scale language models.

2. **Pretraining**:
   - GPT models are **pretrained** on vast amounts of text data in an unsupervised fashion. During this phase, the model learns to predict the next word in a sentence given the context of previous words. This allows it to capture the statistical relationships between words, sentence structures, and linguistic patterns.
   - Pretraining is done in a **language modeling** setting, where the model is exposed to billions of sentences and learns to predict the likelihood of the next word or token. This gives GPT the ability to generate coherent and contextually appropriate text based on a given prompt.

3. **Fine-Tuning**:
   - After pretraining, GPT models can be **fine-tuned** for specific tasks by training on smaller, task-specific datasets. For example, GPT can be fine-tuned for tasks like **question answering**, **summarization**, or **translation** by training it on labeled datasets that contain input-output pairs.
   - Fine-tuning allows the model to specialize in particular tasks, improving performance for those specific applications.

4. **Decoder-Only Architecture**:

- GPT models use a **decoder-only** architecture, which means they generate output one token at a time based on previous tokens in the sequence. The model starts with a prompt and predicts the next word in the sequence, iterating this process until it completes the sentence or paragraph.
- In contrast, some transformer models (like **BERT**) use an **encoder-decoder** architecture, where the encoder processes input and the decoder generates output. GPT, however, focuses purely on decoding and generating sequential text.

How GPT-3 and GPT-4 Work and Their Impact

1. **How GPT-3 Works**:
   - GPT-3 works by using **prompt-based generation**. When a user provides a prompt (e.g., "Write a story about a dragon"), GPT-3 processes this input and generates text by predicting one word at a time, considering the context of the previous words. GPT-3 can generate long-form content such as articles, essays, and code, all while maintaining coherence and relevance to the initial prompt.
   - The model leverages its vast size (175 billion parameters) to generate fluent, contextually appropriate text across a wide range of tasks, such as answering

questions, completing sentences, and even performing basic arithmetic.

2. **How GPT-4 Works**:
   o GPT-4 builds on GPT-3's success by incorporating multimodal capabilities. This means that GPT-4 can process both text and images as input, making it more versatile in handling complex tasks that require understanding of both visual and textual information.
   o GPT-4's large scale and improved algorithms allow it to generate even more creative and accurate responses, with better factual accuracy and less likelihood of producing harmful or biased content.
   o GPT-4's ability to handle more nuanced instructions and engage in complex reasoning tasks is a significant improvement, making it even more useful for applications that require deeper understanding and problem-solving.

Real-World Example: Using GPT for Creative Writing and Content Creation

GPT-3 and GPT-4 have made significant strides in automating and augmenting creative writing and content creation. Here's how these models are being used in the real world:

1. **Content Generation**:

- GPT models are widely used in the marketing and media industries to generate **blog posts, articles, ad copy**, and **social media content**. With minimal input (e.g., a headline or brief prompt), GPT can produce high-quality, coherent, and engaging content that matches the tone and style requested by the user.
- For example, **Copy.ai** and **Jasper.ai** are platforms that leverage GPT-3 to generate content for businesses, enabling them to scale content production while maintaining quality.

2. **Creative Writing**:
    - Writers and authors use GPT-3 as a tool to brainstorm ideas, generate plotlines, or even co-write stories. By providing a prompt, the model can suggest new directions for a narrative or write entire chapters that align with the writer's style.
    - GPT-3 has also been used for **poetry generation**, creating poems based on a given theme, emotional tone, or stylistic request.

3. **Personalized Content**:
    - GPT-3 and GPT-4 can generate **personalized** content based on user input, allowing for tailored newsletters, product descriptions, and even personalized fiction. This level of customization makes GPT models highly valuable for companies in fields like **e-commerce**, **advertising**, and **customer engagement**.

Summary

In this chapter, we explored the evolution of **GPT models**, from **GPT-1** to **GPT-4**, and how they have revolutionized text generation. GPT models are based on the **Transformer architecture**, which uses self-attention mechanisms to process text efficiently and capture long-range dependencies. We also discussed how GPT-3 and GPT-4 work, with GPT-4 incorporating multimodal capabilities and improved reasoning.

Finally, we delved into real-world applications of GPT for **creative writing** and **content creation**, highlighting how these models are transforming industries by automating and enhancing the creative process. As we move forward, we'll dive deeper into how these tools can be applied in various domains, empowering creativity and productivity in unprecedented ways.

CHAPTER SIX

Fine-Tuning GPT Models

What is Fine-Tuning and Why Does it Matter?

Fine-tuning refers to the process of taking a pre-trained model (such as GPT-3 or GPT-4) and adapting it to a specific task or domain by training it further on a smaller, more targeted dataset. This allows the model to leverage the knowledge it has already gained during the pretraining phase (from large-scale data) while specializing in the particular nuances of the new task at hand.

The key advantage of fine-tuning is that it allows for **task-specific optimization**. While the pre-trained GPT models are incredibly powerful, their generality means they are often not perfectly suited for specialized tasks like customer support, legal advice, or medical diagnostics. By fine-tuning the model, you enable it to perform better on a narrower range of tasks, enhancing its effectiveness and relevance.

Here's why fine-tuning matters:

1. **Task Specialization**: Fine-tuning allows GPT models to specialize in a given domain, such as customer service, legal contracts, or creative writing, enabling the model to generate more accurate and contextually relevant responses.

2. **Improved Performance**: Fine-tuned models tend to outperform their general pre-trained counterparts in specific tasks, especially when they are trained on high-quality, task-specific data. This leads to better user experiences and more efficient solutions.

3. **Cost and Time Efficiency**: Fine-tuning saves significant time and computational resources. Instead of training a new model from scratch (which would be costly and time-consuming), you can fine-tune an existing model, building on the foundational knowledge it already has.

4. **Customization**: Fine-tuning allows you to customize a model to fit your specific needs. For example, you can train the model on customer interactions to make it more adept at handling specific types of questions and situations.

How to Fine-Tune GPT Models for Specific Tasks

Fine-tuning a GPT model typically involves the following steps:

1. **Data Collection and Preparation**:
   o The first step in fine-tuning is gathering and preparing the relevant dataset. This dataset should be representative of the task or domain you want the model to specialize in. For example, if you're fine-tuning GPT for customer support, your

dataset should consist of real customer queries and appropriate responses.

- The data must be cleaned and formatted for use in training. This may include removing irrelevant information, ensuring text consistency, and organizing the data into input-output pairs that are easily digestible for the model.

2. **Training Setup**:

- Once the dataset is ready, you need to set up the fine-tuning process. This involves selecting the pre-trained model (e.g., GPT-3 or GPT-4) and specifying the hyperparameters for the fine-tuning process, such as the learning rate, batch size, and number of training epochs.
- During fine-tuning, the model will adjust its internal parameters to better align with the specific task. Fine-tuning GPT typically involves **supervised learning**, where the model learns by matching inputs to desired outputs based on your dataset.

3. **Training the Model**:

- Fine-tuning is done by continuing the training process on the new dataset. The model is provided with examples from your data, and it gradually learns to generate the correct output for a given input.
- It's important to monitor the training process to avoid overfitting (where the model becomes too specific to the fine-

tuning data and performs poorly on new data). Techniques like **early stopping** or **regularization** are used to prevent this.

4. **Evaluation and Testing**:
   - After fine-tuning, the model's performance is evaluated using a test dataset (a separate dataset that wasn't seen during training). This allows you to check if the model has successfully adapted to the new task and if it generalizes well to unseen data.
   - Depending on the results, you may need to iterate on the fine-tuning process by adjusting the model's hyperparameters, improving the dataset, or adding more examples.

5. **Deployment**:
   - Once the model is fine-tuned and tested, it can be deployed for use in real-world applications. This could be as a customer support chatbot, a writing assistant, or a document summarizer, depending on the fine-tuning task.
   - Deployment often involves integrating the fine-tuned model into a web or mobile application, or using APIs for real-time interaction with users.

Real-World Example: Fine-Tuning GPT for Customer Support Chatbots

One of the most common applications of fine-tuning GPT models is in the creation of **customer support chatbots**. Many companies are now using AI-driven chatbots to handle customer inquiries, automate support processes, and enhance user experiences. Fine-tuning GPT for this purpose can help the chatbot better understand the company's products, services, and specific customer queries.

Here's how you might go about fine-tuning GPT for a customer support chatbot:

1. **Step 1: Data Collection**:
    o You begin by collecting a dataset of **real customer support conversations**. This could include chat logs, email exchanges, or transcriptions of phone conversations. It's important to have a diverse set of examples that cover a range of topics, such as account inquiries, product troubleshooting, billing questions, and general customer service requests.
    o You may also want to include responses from human agents to ensure the chatbot learns the appropriate tone and context.
2. **Step 2: Preprocessing**:
    o The collected data needs to be cleaned and formatted into a structured dataset. For example, each customer query and its corresponding response would be treated

as a pair of **input-output** examples. This could be as simple as a **question-answer pair** or a more complex **conversation** where the model must maintain context over multiple exchanges.

3. **Step 3: Fine-Tuning the Model**:
   - Once the data is ready, the fine-tuning process begins. You would use GPT (e.g., GPT-3 or GPT-4) and train it on your customer support data. This process teaches the model how to handle customer queries in a way that matches your company's tone, style, and knowledge base.
   - Fine-tuning might also include training the model on handling **escalation scenarios**, where the bot needs to recognize when to hand off a conversation to a human agent.

4. **Step 4: Testing the Chatbot**:
   - After fine-tuning, it's essential to test the chatbot in real-world scenarios. This testing involves providing it with new customer queries and evaluating the quality of its responses. The chatbot should be able to understand a wide variety of questions and provide relevant answers in a coherent, professional manner.
   - Testing should also focus on ensuring that the bot handles edge cases effectively and that it can escalate complex issues to human agents when necessary.

5. **Step 5: Deployment**:
    o After successful fine-tuning and testing, the chatbot is ready for deployment. It can be integrated into your company's website, app, or other customer-facing platforms where customers can interact with it.
    o Once deployed, the chatbot can be continuously monitored to ensure it is performing well. You can also fine-tune the model further with new data to improve its performance over time.

Summary

In this chapter, we explored **fine-tuning GPT models**, which involves adapting a pre-trained model to perform a specific task or domain by training it on a specialized dataset. Fine-tuning allows GPT models to excel in applications like customer support chatbots, where the model must understand specific products, services, and user queries.

We also walked through the **step-by-step process** of fine-tuning a GPT model, from data collection and preprocessing to training, testing, and deployment. As demonstrated by the **customer support chatbot** example, fine-tuning allows GPT models to deliver more accurate, contextually relevant, and human-like responses, significantly improving customer service automation.

Fine-tuning plays a crucial role in making large pre-trained models like GPT more effective and applicable to a wide range of real-world scenarios. As we continue to explore generative AI, fine-tuning will remain an essential tool for tailoring models to specific tasks and industries.

CHAPTER SEVEN

Text-to-Image Generation: The Birth of DALL·E

Introduction to Text-to-Image Models

Text-to-image generation refers to the process of generating images from textual descriptions using artificial intelligence (AI). The concept is a part of **multimodal AI**, where models are capable of processing and generating different types of data, such as text, images, and audio. Text-to-image models are designed to bridge the gap between language and vision, allowing users to input descriptive text, and the AI will create an image that matches the description.

For example, a user could input a phrase like "a futuristic city skyline at sunset," and the AI would generate a realistic or artistic image that aligns with that description. This process leverages both **Natural Language Processing (NLP)** for understanding the text and **Computer Vision (CV)** for image creation, making it one of the most exciting applications of generative AI.

The significance of text-to-image models goes beyond simple image generation. These models allow for creativity, democratizing access to design, art, and visual storytelling, and offering a new way for non-experts to create visual content using only text.

How DALL·E Generates Images from Text Descriptions

DALL·E is an advanced text-to-image model developed by **OpenAI**. The model is built on a transformer-based architecture similar to **GPT**, but instead of generating text, it generates images. Here's how it works:

1. **Training**:
   - DALL·E is trained on a massive dataset of image-text pairs, meaning each image is accompanied by a descriptive caption. During training, DALL·E learns the relationships between text and visual content, allowing it to understand how specific words and phrases map to particular visual features.
   - The model learns to associate objects, scenes, colors, textures, and other visual elements with corresponding textual descriptions. This allows it to generate images that are consistent with the input description.
2. **The Encoding and Decoding Process**:
   - When given a text prompt, DALL·E processes the input in a similar way to **GPT**. The text is first tokenized into a format the model can understand, and these tokens are then mapped to a latent space—a compressed representation of the text.
   - Using this latent representation, DALL·E generates an image by decoding the

information into a high-dimensional visual representation. The model outputs pixels that form a coherent image that aligns with the input description.

- The process is guided by the attention mechanism, which helps the model focus on specific parts of the text while generating the image. For example, the word "sunset" would guide the model to generate a sky with the appropriate colors, while the word "futuristic" could influence the architectural style of buildings in the image.

3. **CLIP (Contrastive Language-Image Pretraining):**

- DALL·E uses **CLIP**, another OpenAI model, to guide the generation process. CLIP is trained to understand both images and text by comparing how well text descriptions match with images. It can help ensure that the images generated by DALL·E match the semantics of the input text, improving coherence and accuracy.

- CLIP works by projecting both images and text into a shared embedding space, allowing the model to compare them directly. This enables DALL·E to generate more relevant and contextually accurate images based on the input text.

4. **Fine-Tuning:**

- After the initial training phase, DALL·E can be fine-tuned for more specific tasks, like generating images in particular styles (e.g., cartoons, realistic art, or abstract designs). Fine-tuning allows DALL·E to generate images that are more tailored to specific creative or commercial needs.

The Importance of Multimodal AI

Multimodal AI refers to the ability of a system to process and generate multiple types of data, such as text, images, and audio. DALL·E and similar models are prime examples of multimodal AI because they integrate both language and vision, allowing them to interpret textual input and produce visual output. Here are a few reasons why multimodal AI is so important:

1. **Enhanced Understanding**:
    o By combining multiple types of data, multimodal AI can have a richer understanding of the world. For example, understanding how text descriptions relate to visual features enables the model to generate images that accurately reflect the meaning and intent behind the words.
    o This cross-modal understanding is not limited to just text and images. Multimodal AI can integrate other types of data, such as sound and video, creating even more immersive and complex AI systems.
2. **Creativity and Design**:
    o Multimodal AI allows for greater creativity by enabling non-experts to

generate high-quality visual content through simple text descriptions. This opens up new possibilities for artists, designers, and creators who may not have traditional graphic design skills but still want to produce professional-level visuals.

- o Text-to-image models like DALL·E make it easier to prototype ideas, generate marketing material, and experiment with design concepts without needing an extensive background in visual arts.

3. **Accessibility**:
   - o Multimodal AI can make creative tools more accessible to people with disabilities. For example, individuals who cannot see or manipulate images can use text-based descriptions to create and interact with visual content.
   - o This democratization of creativity enables a broader group of people to contribute to visual art, design, and digital media production, further pushing the boundaries of innovation.

4. **Real-World Application Across Domains**:
   - o Multimodal AI has applications in a variety of domains beyond art and design, including **healthcare**, **education**, **entertainment**, and **marketing**. For example, in healthcare, models like DALL·E can generate medical illustrations based on text descriptions to help explain complex concepts. In

entertainment, it could generate visual effects or scene layouts from screenplay descriptions.

Real-World Example: Creating Art and Designs with DALL·E

One of the most exciting applications of DALL·E is its ability to create art and designs from text prompts, allowing artists, designers, and marketers to generate unique visuals without requiring advanced design skills. Here's how DALL·E can be used in the real world:

1. **Creative Art and Illustration**:
   - Artists and graphic designers can use DALL·E to generate illustrations based on detailed text descriptions. For example, an artist might input a prompt like "A serene landscape with a calm lake, surrounded by tall mountains and a colorful sunset," and DALL·E would generate an image that matches this description, offering inspiration or even a completed piece of art.
   - DALL·E can also help artists explore different styles and compositions quickly. If a designer wants to experiment with a particular aesthetic (e.g., "Art Deco style") or specific colors, they can provide a description, and DALL·E will generate images in that style.
2. **Marketing and Advertising**:

- In marketing, DALL·E can be used to create promotional materials like banners, posters, or social media graphics. For instance, a marketing team could input a text description like "A stylish, modern coffee shop with neon lights and a cozy atmosphere" and generate images for use in advertising campaigns.
- This can be particularly useful for rapid prototyping, where marketers can quickly generate multiple visual concepts to evaluate different design ideas without needing to hire a designer for each new concept.

3. **Product Design**:
   - Product designers can also leverage DALL·E to generate ideas for new products. For example, a fashion designer could input a description like "A futuristic jacket with glowing accents" and get a range of design options to spark further creative development.
   - DALL·E can help designers explore variations of products based on specific features, styles, or materials described in the prompt, making it an invaluable tool for brainstorming and conceptualization.

4. **Content Creation for Social Media**:
   - Content creators on platforms like Instagram, YouTube, and TikTok can use DALL·E to generate visually striking content based on a simple text prompt. For instance, a creator might ask DALL·E

to generate an image of "a vibrant cityscape filled with neon signs and flying cars," which can then be used as the backdrop for a social media post or video thumbnail.

o This allows for rapid, high-quality visual content creation, saving creators time and providing them with creative visuals that align with their brand identity or theme.

Summary

In this chapter, we explored the exciting field of **text-to-image generation** and how models like **DALL·E** have brought about a revolution in creative content generation. We discussed how DALL·E generates images from text descriptions, leveraging the power of multimodal AI to combine language and vision for more effective and creative applications.

From creating artwork and designs to developing marketing materials and product concepts, **text-to-image models** have made visual content creation more accessible and efficient than ever before. DALL·E and other models in this space are democratizing the ability to generate high-quality visuals, offering new opportunities for creators across multiple industries.

As text-to-image generation continues to improve, the potential applications are virtually limitless, from gaming and entertainment to education, healthcare, and beyond. These advancements are transforming how we interact with AI and creativity, paving the way for an entirely new era of content creation.

CHAPTER EIGHT

Stable Diffusion: Democratizing Image Generation

Introduction to Stable Diffusion and its Technology

Stable Diffusion is an advanced image generation model that has gained significant attention for its ability to generate high-quality images from text prompts. Released by **Stability AI** in 2022, Stable Diffusion is a powerful, open-source **text-to-image** model that enables users to generate stunning, realistic, or artistic images based on simple text descriptions. Unlike previous proprietary models like **DALL·E** or **MidJourney**, Stable Diffusion stands out because it is open-source, allowing developers, artists, and creators to customize and integrate it into their projects without the need for expensive API access or specialized hardware.

What sets Stable Diffusion apart is not just its ability to generate impressive images, but its **democratizing effect** on image generation. Because the model is available for free and can be run on consumer-level hardware (with a decent GPU), it opens up new opportunities for individuals and smaller businesses who may not have had access to these powerful tools before.

Stable Diffusion operates using a **latent diffusion model (LDM)**, which significantly reduces the computational cost of generating high-quality images compared to earlier methods like GANs or traditional diffusion models. This model makes it possible for users to create images at scale while keeping the process efficient and accessible.

How Stable Diffusion Works: Latent Diffusion Models Explained

The core technology behind Stable Diffusion is the **latent diffusion model (LDM),** which is designed to make the process of generating images from text more efficient. Here's how it works:

1. **Latent Space and Image Compression**:
    o   Instead of operating directly in the pixel space, where every pixel of an image is explicitly generated, Stable Diffusion works in a **latent space**—a compressed, lower-dimensional representation of the image. This is a key innovation that allows the model to generate images more quickly and efficiently while still retaining high quality.
    o   The **encoder** of the model takes the input image and compresses it into this latent space, where the model can manipulate the data without needing to directly handle the pixel data, reducing the computational complexity.
2. **Diffusion Process**:

- o Stable Diffusion uses a process called **diffusion**, which involves gradually adding noise to an image and then reversing this process to denoise and generate a new image. During the diffusion process, noise is introduced to an image (starting from random noise), and the model learns to iteratively reduce this noise, effectively reconstructing an image that fits the given text description.
- o This iterative process is what gives Stable Diffusion its name: it diffuses the noise through several steps until a clean image emerges, closely aligned with the description.

3. **Text-to-Image Generation**:
- o To generate an image from text, Stable Diffusion uses a combination of the **text encoder** and the diffusion process. The **text encoder** (usually based on a pretrained model like **CLIP** or a similar text-to-image model) takes the input text and converts it into a representation that the diffusion model can understand.
- o The model then starts from a noise-filled image and uses the text encoding to guide the denoising process, gradually refining the image to match the description provided. This process is repeated multiple times until the final, detailed image is produced.

4. **Fine-Tuning and Customization**:

- o One of the powerful features of Stable Diffusion is its ability to be **fine-tuned** for specific tasks or domains. Artists and developers can train the model on specialized datasets to generate images in particular styles (e.g., anime, architectural renderings, or photorealistic images).
- o This customization ability makes Stable Diffusion a versatile tool for a wide range of creative applications, from art and design to product prototyping and marketing.

Comparison with Other Image Generation Models (e.g., DALL·E, MidJourney)

While Stable Diffusion has quickly gained popularity, it's important to understand how it compares to other well-known image generation models like **DALL·E** and **MidJourney**. Let's compare their key differences:

1. **DALL·E:**
   - o **Developed by OpenAI, DALL·E** (currently at version 2) is one of the most well-known text-to-image models. It generates images based on textual descriptions, with impressive accuracy and creativity.
   - o **Key Feature**: DALL·E is known for its ability to generate highly creative and surreal images that combine various concepts (e.g., "a futuristic car made of

flowers"). It uses a **transformer-based architecture** and was trained on a vast dataset of image-text pairs.

o **Difference with Stable Diffusion**: DALL·E operates on a larger scale and uses more computational resources. Unlike Stable Diffusion, which operates in a latent space and is highly efficient, DALL·E runs directly in the pixel space, making it more resource-intensive.

2. **MidJourney**:

o **MidJourney** is another popular text-to-image generation model, known for its highly artistic and stylized images. MidJourney is particularly favored by artists and designers for its unique aesthetic, which is often characterized by a more abstract, painterly style.

o **Key Feature**: MidJourney emphasizes creativity and artistry, making it ideal for generating visually stunning and imaginative pieces.

o **Difference with Stable Diffusion**: While MidJourney generates beautiful images, it is a **closed-source** platform, and users must subscribe to access its tools. Stable Diffusion, by contrast, is **open-source**, allowing broader access and customization.

3. **Stable Diffusion**:

o **Key Feature**: Stable Diffusion offers a **unique combination** of efficiency, quality, and flexibility. By operating in the latent space, it generates images more quickly and with fewer computational resources compared to DALL·E and other models. It is also open-source, enabling developers to fine-tune and adapt the model for specific creative tasks.

○ **Flexibility**: Stable Diffusion is highly customizable. Because it's open-source, users can train the model with their own datasets or fine-tune it to produce images in specific styles (e.g., hyperrealism, fantasy, or abstract art). This ability to adapt the model makes it particularly useful for professionals in design, marketing, and entertainment.

Real-World Example: Using Stable Diffusion for Creative Projects

One of the most exciting applications of Stable Diffusion is in the **creative industries**, where it is transforming the way art, design, and content are generated. Here's a real-world example of how Stable Diffusion can be used for creative projects:

1. **Creating Marketing Materials**:
   ○ A **marketing team** for a fashion brand wants to generate new advertising visuals for their upcoming collection. Instead of hiring an illustrator or graphic designer to create each piece of visual content, the team uses Stable Diffusion to generate a

variety of visual concepts based on specific text prompts.

- o For example, they might input the prompt: "A modern fashion collection set in a neon-lit futuristic city." Stable Diffusion will generate several stunning, high-quality images in a matter of seconds, giving the marketing team multiple design options to choose from.
- o This process allows for rapid **ideation** and **prototyping**, reducing the time and cost traditionally required for visual content creation.

2. **Concept Art for Video Games**:
- o Game developers can use Stable Diffusion to generate **concept art** for characters, environments, and story scenes. A prompt like "A mysterious forest with glowing plants and magical creatures" would generate a range of beautiful, imaginative images for the game's visual direction.
- o These images can serve as the basis for further development or be directly used as assets in the game, speeding up the process of creating visual content and giving developers more creative options to work with.

3. **Graphic Design for Illustrations**:
- o Independent **artists and illustrators** can use Stable Diffusion as a **creative tool** to enhance their workflow. By inputting specific prompts, artists can generate

initial drafts of images, then refine them further based on their own artistic vision.

- o For instance, an artist might provide a description like "A digital painting of a dragon flying over a castle at sunset" and receive multiple stunning drafts of that scene. The artist can then take these drafts and modify them further, adding unique details or blending them with their own style.

4. **Product Design and Prototyping**:
   - o Product designers can use Stable Diffusion to generate visual prototypes of new products or concepts. For example, a designer working on a new tech gadget can input a prompt like "A sleek, futuristic smartwatch with holographic display" and receive multiple design variations.
   - o This allows product teams to explore different design possibilities without needing to create each prototype manually, facilitating faster development and more creative product ideas.

Summary

In this chapter, we explored **Stable Diffusion**, an open-source **text-to-image** model that has made image generation more accessible and democratized for creators across various industries. We discussed how

Stable Diffusion works using **latent diffusion models**, which offer a more computationally efficient way to generate high-quality images compared to traditional diffusion models or GANs.

We also compared Stable Diffusion with other image generation models like **DALL·E** and **MidJourney**, highlighting its open-source nature, efficiency, and flexibility. Finally, we explored how Stable Diffusion is used in real-world creative projects, such as marketing, game design, and product prototyping, demonstrating its versatility and potential in revolutionizing the creative process.

As Stable Diffusion continues to evolve and gain popularity, its role in empowering creators and businesses will only grow, offering limitless possibilities for generating high-quality visual content quickly and efficiently.

CHAPTER NINE

MidJourney and Other Image Generators

Overview of MidJourney and Other Competitors

MidJourney is a widely popular AI tool that generates images from text prompts, much like Stable Diffusion and DALL·E. Known for its distinctive and highly artistic style, MidJourney is favored by artists, designers, and creative professionals for its ability to generate visually stunning and abstract images. It excels in creating art that has an almost ethereal or surreal quality, making it a top choice for projects that require creativity and innovation.

Launched as a closed platform, MidJourney operates on a **subscription model** and provides users with access to a powerful AI tool for creating art, illustrations, and design concepts. Unlike Stable Diffusion, which is open-source, MidJourney is a proprietary service. Users interact with MidJourney via a Discord bot, entering text prompts to generate artwork in various styles.

Other **image-generating competitors** to MidJourney include:

1. **DALL·E 2**:
   - Developed by **OpenAI, DALL·E 2** is another highly effective text-to-image model. Known for its versatility, DALL·E

2 can generate images from detailed prompts, including surreal or imaginative combinations. DALL·E 2 also offers the ability to edit generated images, a feature known as **inpainting**, allowing users to make specific alterations to parts of an image.

o Unlike MidJourney, DALL·E 2 is more balanced in terms of realism and abstraction, making it suitable for a wide variety of use cases, from commercial advertisements to personal creative projects.

2. **Artbreeder**:

o **Artbreeder** is a platform that uses AI to blend and morph existing images based on user inputs. It focuses heavily on genetic algorithms and allows users to create images by combining different "genes" or features of various images. Artbreeder is especially popular among character designers and people creating fantasy or science fiction art, as it allows for the creation of faces, landscapes, and other visuals that evolve through iterative processes.

3. **DeepAI**:

o **DeepAI** offers several AI tools, including a text-to-image generator. DeepAI's image generation capabilities are more straightforward than those of MidJourney and DALL·E 2 but still provide a valuable resource for artists and developers. Their

API-based services allow businesses and individuals to easily integrate AI-driven image creation into their own workflows.

4. **RunwayML**:
   o **RunwayML** is another powerful creative platform that offers AI tools for generating images, videos, and other creative assets. RunwayML includes **text-to-image** generation as part of its suite, and it's favored for its **user-friendly interface** that simplifies the process of creating and editing AI-generated content. The platform is popular for its **integration with Adobe tools** and for being accessible to users without coding skills.

The Differences Between Diffusion Models and GANs

Two popular approaches to generating images with AI are **diffusion models** (like Stable Diffusion and DALL·E 2) and **Generative Adversarial Networks (GANs)**. While both can generate realistic and creative images, they operate in fundamentally different ways. Here's a breakdown of their core differences:

1. **Generative Adversarial Networks (GANs)**:
   o **GANs** were introduced by **Ian Goodfellow** in 2014 and have become one of the most widely used methods for generating images. They consist of two main components:

- **Generator**: The generator creates synthetic data (e.g., an image).
- **Discriminator**: The discriminator evaluates the generated data and distinguishes between real and fake data.

o The generator and discriminator are trained together in an adversarial setup, where the generator tries to fool the discriminator by generating increasingly realistic data, while the discriminator tries to improve at detecting fake data. This results in the generator improving over time and creating highly realistic images.

o **Advantages of GANs**: GANs are capable of generating highly detailed images with fine textures, often making them ideal for tasks like photo-realistic image generation.

o **Disadvantages of GANs**: GANs can be prone to issues like **mode collapse**, where the generator produces limited diversity in its outputs, and they can be difficult to train effectively, requiring careful tuning.

2. **Diffusion Models**:

o **Diffusion models** (like Stable Diffusion) work by iteratively adding noise to an image and then learning to reverse this process, effectively denoising the image. Starting with random noise, the model gradually refines the image, creating a final output that aligns with the input text description.

- o **Advantages of Diffusion Models**: Diffusion models are more stable and easier to train than GANs. They also tend to generate more diverse outputs, as they do not suffer from the same mode collapse issues that GANs do.
- o **Disadvantages of Diffusion Models**: While the quality of images generated by diffusion models is very high, the generation process can be slower than GANs, as it requires more computational steps to refine the image.

In summary, **GANs** tend to generate images more quickly and are excellent for producing photorealistic details, but they are more prone to training instability. **Diffusion models**, on the other hand, are more stable, produce higher-quality images, and offer better diversity, but they require more time to generate each image.

Practical Applications for Artists and Designers

AI-driven image generation tools like MidJourney, Stable Diffusion, and others have become invaluable assets for **artists and designers**, offering new creative possibilities and streamlining workflows. Here's how these tools are being used in the creative industry:

1. **Concept Art for Films and Games**:

- o Artists and game designers use AI tools to quickly generate **concept art** for characters, environments, and scenes. This allows for faster prototyping and experimentation with different visual ideas before committing to detailed, time-consuming designs.
- o For example, a concept artist for a **sci-fi film** might use MidJourney or DALL·E 2 to generate initial concepts of futuristic landscapes, alien creatures, or spaceship designs based on text descriptions.

2. **Advertising and Branding**:
   - o Marketers and designers use AI tools to create engaging visuals for campaigns, product ads, and social media posts. These tools allow them to generate custom images tailored to specific campaigns or branding requirements.
   - o With just a prompt like "luxury watch on a reflective surface with a minimalist background," designers can quickly generate high-quality visuals for use in advertising materials, avoiding the time and expense of traditional photoshoots.

3. **Illustration and Editorial Art**:
   - o Illustrators use text-to-image generation tools to create original illustrations for books, magazines, websites, and more. By inputting descriptive prompts, artists can generate artwork that aligns with the style and mood of a story or article.

- o AI-generated illustrations are also used in **children's books** and **editorial cartoons**, where the flexibility of text prompts allows for tailored and unique illustrations that resonate with specific audiences.

4. **Fashion and Product Design**:
   - o Fashion designers use image generation tools to visualize new clothing lines, color schemes, and accessory concepts. With AI, they can quickly prototype different designs without having to sketch them by hand or rely on traditional digital design software.
   - o Similarly, product designers can use AI tools to create early-stage designs for gadgets, furniture, and packaging, allowing them to explore multiple iterations and variations quickly.

Real-World Example: How Designers Use AI Tools for Concept Art

Let's look at a **real-world example** of how designers can use AI tools like **MidJourney** and **Stable Diffusion** for creating **concept art**.

Imagine a video game development studio working on a new open-world role-playing game (RPG). The art team needs to generate concept art for different locations within the game, such as ancient temples, lush forests, and futuristic cities. Instead of spending weeks or months on each concept, the designers use AI tools to generate multiple concepts based on textual prompts.

1. **Step 1: Generating Ideas**:
   o The lead designer inputs a prompt into MidJourney: "A mysterious ancient temple hidden deep in a jungle, with large stone steps and intricate carvings on the walls." Within minutes, MidJourney generates several high-quality concept images of the temple, with varying perspectives and styles.
   o The team reviews the images, picking elements they like (e.g., the detailed carvings or the lighting) and providing new prompts to refine the designs further.
2. **Step 2: Refining the Concept**:
   o After selecting the most promising images, the designer refines the concept by inputting a new prompt like "sunlight filtering through the trees, casting shadows on the temple's entrance" to adjust the lighting and atmosphere.
   o With this new description, the AI generates several more images with the desired changes, providing the team with a more focused visual direction.
3. **Step 3: Finalizing the Design**:
   o Once the designers are satisfied with the concept art, they use it as a basis for creating detailed 3D models and textures for the game. AI-generated concept art saves the team significant time in the

initial stages of development, enabling them to quickly explore different ideas before diving into detailed design work.

By using AI tools like MidJourney and Stable Diffusion, designers can rapidly generate and iterate on creative concepts, speeding up the creative process and allowing for more innovation and experimentation in game design, film production, and other creative industries.

Summary

In this chapter, we explored **MidJourney** and other **image generation models** like **DALL·E** and **Stable Diffusion**. We discussed how these models differ from each other, particularly in terms of their underlying technology—**diffusion models** versus **GANs**—and how they are reshaping the creative industries by offering new ways for artists and designers to generate high-quality images from text descriptions.

We also looked at the **practical applications** of these AI tools for artists and designers, from concept art for games and movies to product design and fashion. By using AI tools, designers can rapidly generate and iterate on creative concepts, saving time and increasing productivity.

As AI continues to advance, the potential for these tools to revolutionize creative workflows is immense, enabling more people to bring their ideas to life and democratizing the world of design.

CHAPTER TEN

Generating Music with AI

AI Models for Music Generation: OpenAI's MuseNet, Jukedeck, etc.

The field of **AI-driven music generation** has seen significant advancements, allowing for the creation of original music tracks, melodies, and compositions based on given inputs or styles. Various AI models have been developed to generate music, with some of the most notable examples being **OpenAI's MuseNet**, **Jukedeck**, and others. These models have expanded the possibilities for music composition, making it easier for both professional musicians and non-experts to create music with the help of artificial intelligence.

1. **OpenAI's MuseNet**:
   - o **MuseNet**, developed by OpenAI, is one of the most well-known AI models for music generation. Trained on a diverse dataset of music spanning several genres, including classical, jazz, pop, and electronic, MuseNet is capable of generating music in a wide variety of styles.
   - o MuseNet works by analyzing and predicting the most likely notes or chords to follow based on the given context. The model can take inputs such as a genre, an

initial melody, or even specific instruments, and generate full-length compositions.

o MuseNet uses a **transformer-based architecture** similar to the one used in GPT models. It learns the patterns in music by observing long sequences of musical data, allowing it to generate complex, multi-instrument compositions.

2. **Jukedeck**:

o **Jukedeck** was an AI platform that focused on generating music specifically for **content creators** like video producers and marketers. The platform used deep learning algorithms to generate royalty-free music based on user inputs such as mood, style, and tempo.

o Jukedeck's primary use case was to provide music for YouTube videos, commercials, and other online content, where creators could easily generate background music without worrying about copyright issues. However, in 2019, Jukedeck was acquired by **TikTok** (then known as ByteDance), and the platform was later shut down as its technology was integrated into TikTok's music-related tools.

3. **Amper Music**:

o **Amper Music** is another AI music generation platform that allows users to create music based on specific parameters, including genre, mood, and tempo. It provides a user-friendly interface where non-musicians can create unique tracks by selecting pre-set styles and customizing them further.

- o Amper Music is designed for businesses, content creators, and filmmakers who need high-quality, customizable music tracks for their projects. It is particularly useful for generating background scores for videos, podcasts, or advertisements.

4. **AIVA (Artificial Intelligence Virtual Artist)**:
   - o **AIVA** is an AI composer that specializes in creating **classical music** and symphonic compositions. Initially designed for the creation of classical music, AIVA has since expanded to other genres, including pop and jazz.
   - o AIVA works by analyzing classical compositions to learn the structure, harmony, and rhythm used by classical composers. It then applies these principles to generate original compositions, which can be used in various artistic contexts.

5. **Soundraw**:
   - o **Soundraw** is an AI music generator designed specifically for content creators. It allows users to create custom music tracks by adjusting parameters like mood, genre, and instruments. Soundraw aims to offer more flexibility by allowing users to collaborate with AI in real-time, making

it an interactive tool for music composition.

o It is particularly useful for creators in need of unique, royalty-free music that fits specific requirements, and it empowers them to control the creative process while still leveraging AI's speed and capabilities.

How AI Can Create Unique Music Tracks

AI models like MuseNet, Jukedeck, and others have the ability to create unique music tracks by using advanced machine learning algorithms to understand patterns in music and then applying those patterns to generate new compositions. Here's how AI can create music:

1. **Learning from Data**:
   o AI music models are trained on large datasets containing diverse genres of music. By analyzing these datasets, the models learn various musical elements, such as melody, harmony, rhythm, and structure.
   o These models capture the relationships between different musical components and learn to predict what comes next in a sequence of notes or chords, making them capable of composing music that follows the same patterns and styles as the data they were trained on.
2. **Generating Music Based on Parameters**:

- AI models can generate music based on **user-defined parameters**, such as genre, mood, tempo, and instruments. For example, a user can specify that they want a "sad piano piece" or a "high-energy pop song," and the AI will generate a track that aligns with those inputs.
- By adjusting these parameters, AI music tools can create a wide range of musical styles, from classical compositions to modern electronic beats, providing creators with nearly infinite possibilities for original music.

3. **Musical Composition and Structure**:
   - Many AI models are capable of composing entire pieces of music, including **melodies**, **harmonies**, and **accompaniments**. They learn the typical structure of a song, such as the arrangement of verses, choruses, and bridges, and use this knowledge to create compositions that flow naturally and are aesthetically pleasing.
   - The AI can also layer multiple instruments together, generating multi-instrument tracks that mimic real-world orchestration or band arrangements. For example, a track might include piano, drums, bass, and strings, each playing their respective roles within the composition.

4. **Interactive Music Creation**:

- o Some AI tools, like **Soundraw**, allow users to interactively collaborate with the AI to create music in real-time. Users can make changes to the music, such as adding or removing instruments, changing the tempo, or adjusting the mood, while the AI adapts the music accordingly. This dynamic interaction gives creators a higher level of control over the output.

5. **Customization and Personalization**:
   - o AI music models can also **personalize** music for specific use cases. For example, AI can tailor music to match the specific themes or emotional tones of a project. A filmmaker could request music for a romantic scene, while a game developer could ask for background music to match a thrilling or dramatic in-game moment.
   - o This customization can be achieved by providing detailed input prompts, allowing the AI to generate tracks that perfectly align with the project's needs.

Real-World Example: Using AI to Create Music for Games, Films, and Commercials

One of the most significant applications of AI-generated music is in the **entertainment and media industries**, where it can be used to create original scores for games, films, commercials, and other content. Here's a real-world example of how AI is used for music creation:

1. **Music for Video Games**:
   - A game development studio working on a role-playing game (RPG) decides to use AI to generate original music for different game levels. The studio uses **Amper Music** or **Soundraw** to create thematic background music for various in-game scenarios—peaceful exploration scenes, intense combat sequences, and suspenseful moments.
   - The AI generates music tracks based on specific parameters (e.g., "upbeat adventure music" or "dark and ominous combat music"), and the development team fine-tunes the tracks to suit the game's pacing and atmosphere. AI allows the team to quickly produce a large variety of music tracks, which would have taken much longer to compose manually.
2. **Film Scores and Soundtracks**:
   - In the film industry, AI tools like **MuseNet** can be used to generate **original scores** for movies and documentaries. For example, a filmmaker working on a historical drama can use MuseNet to generate a classical music score that fits the tone and setting of the film.
   - The film's composer might input a prompt like "orchestral music for an epic battle scene" into the AI system, and MuseNet generates a full orchestral composition with strings, brass, and

percussion that can be used in the soundtrack. The AI music can then be further customized and refined to match the filmmaker's vision.

3. **Music for Commercials and Advertisements**:
   o AI-generated music is also becoming increasingly popular in the advertising world. Brands can use AI tools to generate **catchy background music** for their advertisements or promotional videos.
   o For instance, an advertisement for a new tech product could use **Jukedeck** or **Amper Music** to create a modern, energetic track that fits the brand's image. The AI system generates multiple variations of the track based on the brand's desired style, mood, and target audience. This gives advertisers a cost-effective and time-efficient way to produce high-quality music for their campaigns.

Summary

In this chapter, we explored how AI is being used to **generate music**, with models like **OpenAI's MuseNet**, **Jukedeck**, and others enabling the creation of unique music tracks for a variety of applications. These AI systems learn from vast datasets of music to create compositions that match specific styles, genres, and moods, making them powerful tools for both professional musicians and non-experts.

We also discussed how AI is being used in **real-world applications** like video games, films, and commercials, providing creative professionals with an efficient and innovative way to produce original music without the need for extensive musical training. AI-generated music is democratizing the music creation process, opening up new possibilities for content creators and professionals in the entertainment industry.

AI's impact on music creation is still growing, and as these models continue to evolve, we can expect even more sophisticated tools for generating music tailored to our unique creative needs.

CHAPTER ELEVEN

Text-to-Video Generation: The Next Frontier

What is Text-to-Video Generation?

Text-to-video generation refers to the process of creating video content directly from textual descriptions using artificial intelligence (AI). Similar to how **text-to-image** models (like **DALL·E** and **Stable Diffusion**) generate still images based on textual prompts, text-to-video models extend this capability to the dynamic realm of video, creating moving visuals from written descriptions. This technology holds the potential to revolutionize industries such as film production, advertising, social media content creation, and virtual reality by offering a faster, more accessible way to create video content.

For example, a user could input a prompt like "A cat running through a field of flowers on a sunny day," and the AI would generate a short video sequence that matches the description—complete with the movement of the cat, the environment of the field, and the lighting of a sunny day.

Text-to-video generation involves several advanced AI techniques, primarily using **deep learning** and **neural networks** that combine elements from **image synthesis**, **motion generation**, and **natural language processing**

(NLP) to produce videos that reflect both the semantics and the visual dynamics of the provided text.

Current Models and Challenges in Video Synthesis

Text-to-video generation is still an emerging area of AI research, and although significant progress has been made, several challenges remain in producing high-quality, coherent videos. Here are the key aspects and challenges associated with text-to-video models:

1. **Models in Text-to-Video Generation**:
   - Some **early-stage models** that are pushing the boundaries of text-to-video generation include **CogVideo, Phenaki**, and **Make-A-Video**. These models are built on the foundation of image-generation models (like those based on GANs and diffusion processes) but introduce temporal consistency and dynamic scene generation to handle motion and video continuity.
   - **CogVideo** (from CogView) is one such model that can generate high-resolution videos from text prompts. It is based on a transformer architecture, similar to GPT models, and uses large-scale datasets to learn the relationship between text descriptions and video sequences.
   - **Make-A-Video** (developed by Meta) is another model that can generate short

videos based on textual descriptions. It extends the capabilities of text-to-image models by introducing video synthesis features, incorporating **motion dynamics, scene transitions**, and **visual continuity** to produce realistic videos from textual input.

2. **Challenges in Video Synthesis**:
   - o **Temporal Consistency**: One of the major challenges in text-to-video generation is ensuring that the video maintains **temporal consistency**. This means that objects, characters, and backgrounds should behave and move in a logical, coherent manner over time, avoiding issues such as flickering, unnatural motion, or scene disjointedness. Ensuring smooth transitions between frames and maintaining consistent object positions and lighting over time is a complex task that goes beyond still image generation.
   - o **Motion and Action Generation**: While creating static images is relatively easier for AI, generating smooth, natural motion in a video is far more challenging. The model must understand how to animate objects, characters, and environments to reflect real-world physics and motion dynamics. For example, when generating a video of a person running, the model needs to understand not just how a person looks but also how their body moves

dynamically in relation to the environment.

- o **Scene and Background Complexity**: Unlike text-to-image generation, where models focus on single static scenes, text-to-video models must handle **dynamic environments**, moving backgrounds, and changes in perspective. Generating a consistent, continuous background (e.g., a city street as a person walks through it) that changes logically as the video progresses is a significant challenge for AI.

- o **Quality and Resolution**: Generating high-resolution videos (in terms of both pixel quality and visual detail) is still a work in progress. Many of the current text-to-video models can create low-resolution video outputs, but generating high-definition videos with realistic textures, fine details, and consistent quality remains an ongoing challenge.

3. **Evaluation and Ethics**:
    - o Evaluating AI-generated video content also poses unique challenges, as traditional quality metrics (such as **FID** for images) may not capture the temporal continuity and motion quality in videos. New evaluation metrics are being proposed to assess how well models generate both the visual aspects and the temporal aspects of videos.

○ Ethical concerns around text-to-video generation also need to be addressed, including issues related to **deepfakes**, **misinformation**, and **content manipulation**. The ability to generate realistic videos from text could be misused for creating harmful or misleading content, so ethical safeguards and proper guidelines for usage are crucial.

Real-World Example: AI in Film and Animation Production

AI's impact on the film and animation industries is already significant, and text-to-video generation is poised to revolutionize these sectors even further. Here's how AI is being used in **film and animation production**:

1. **Film and Visual Effects (VFX)**:
   ○ In the film industry, AI-driven video generation tools can be used to create **conceptual scenes**, **storyboard animations**, and even **rough drafts** of sequences based on script descriptions. This can significantly speed up the **pre-production** process, allowing filmmakers to quickly visualize scenes without waiting for costly, time-consuming manual labor.

- o Imagine a filmmaker writing a script where they describe an alien spaceship landing in a desolate desert. With text-to-video generation, the filmmaker could input the description, and the AI would create a rough video mockup of the scene—complete with the spaceship, the desert, and appropriate lighting and textures—giving the team a visual starting point for further refinement.

2. **Animation Production**:
   - o Text-to-video models are particularly powerful for **animation** because they can generate dynamic scenes without the need to manually draw each frame. An animator might describe a scene where a character performs a series of actions (e.g., "a young girl dancing with flowing red ribbons under a full moon") and the AI can generate an animated video of the scene.
   - o This technology could reduce the time and cost involved in producing animated sequences, especially for independent filmmakers or small studios without large animation teams. The AI-generated animation can serve as the foundation for final editing, voiceovers, and additional effects.

3. **Music Videos and Commercials**:
   - o Text-to-video generation is also being used in the creation of **music videos** and **commercials**, where AI can quickly

generate video content based on the lyrics of a song or the description of a brand's message.

- o For example, a music producer can input a song's lyrics into a text-to-video model, and the AI can generate an abstract or narrative-driven video that matches the emotional tone and content of the song. This allows for rapid creation of video content for artists and brands with minimal reliance on traditional video production teams.

4. **Virtual Reality (VR) and Augmented Reality (AR):**
   - o Text-to-video generation can also be applied in the **VR/AR** industry, where immersive virtual environments and characters are created based on textual prompts. For instance, a game developer can input a description of a fantasy world, and the AI can generate both the 3D video and the dynamic elements required to bring that world to life in virtual reality.
   - o This offers exciting possibilities for creating interactive experiences, where users can provide prompts that shape the story, environment, or narrative in real-time.

Summary

In this chapter, we explored **text-to-video generation**, an emerging field within AI that holds the potential to revolutionize industries like **film production**, **animation**, **advertising**, and **virtual reality**. By generating videos directly from text descriptions, this technology simplifies the video production process, enabling rapid prototyping, creative experimentation, and accessibility for creators across various sectors.

We also discussed the **challenges** in video synthesis, such as **temporal consistency**, **motion generation**, and **scene complexity**, as well as the models currently pushing the boundaries of text-to-video generation, including **CogVideo**, **Phenaki**, and **Make-A-Video**.

Real-world applications, particularly in **film**, **animation**, and **music video production**, are already underway, with AI playing a key role in speeding up creative workflows and enabling content creators to bring their ideas to life more efficiently.

As the technology continues to develop, text-to-video generation will likely become an indispensable tool for filmmakers, animators, advertisers, and other creative professionals, making video content creation more dynamic, affordable, and accessible than ever before.

CHAPTER TWELVE

Using Generative AI for Creativity in Gaming

The Role of AI in Game Design

Generative AI has become an invaluable tool in the world of game development, offering innovative ways to enhance the creative process. Traditionally, game design involved manual work by artists, designers, and developers who meticulously crafted game assets, levels, characters, and storylines. However, AI is now helping to automate and accelerate many of these tasks, allowing developers to focus on the overarching game experience rather than spending time on repetitive or time-consuming tasks.

AI in Game Design can serve several roles, from enhancing player experiences to streamlining game development workflows:

1. **Automating Asset Creation**:
   o AI can generate **3D models, textures, animations**, and **sound effects**, significantly reducing the time it takes to create these assets manually. For example, AI models can quickly generate realistic or stylized environments, characters, and objects, ensuring consistency and quality in the game world.

2. **Procedural Content Generation**:
   - AI-powered systems, particularly **procedural generation**, can create vast game worlds, characters, and scenarios dynamically. This is particularly beneficial in open-world games or games that require large-scale, diverse environments.
3. **Enhancing Storytelling and Narrative Design**:
   - AI can assist in creating dynamic, **branching storylines** by generating quests, dialogue, and character interactions based on player choices. This allows for the development of highly interactive and personalized gameplay experiences where the narrative adapts in response to the player's actions.
4. **Level and Environment Design**:
   - **Level design** is a critical aspect of game development. AI can help create dynamic levels by analyzing patterns in existing levels or generating new ones using procedural algorithms. It can also adapt levels in real-time based on player performance, ensuring a challenging but rewarding experience.
5. **Improving NPC Behavior and AI Companions**:
   - AI also plays a role in **non-playable characters (NPCs)** and companions, enhancing their behavior to be more realistic and reactive to the player. By leveraging **reinforcement learning** and

natural language processing (NLP), NPCs can engage in more fluid and interactive conversations with players, adapting their actions and responses based on the player's decisions.

How AI Can Generate Game Assets, Levels, and Stories

1. **Generating Game Assets**:
   - **Generative Adversarial Networks (GANs)** and **Variational Autoencoders (VAEs)** can be used to generate realistic 3D models and textures for characters, environments, and objects. These models can be trained on existing data (such as 3D models or scanned real-world objects) to learn the patterns, styles, and characteristics needed to create new assets that blend seamlessly into the game world.
   - **Example**: In **Minecraft**, AI could be used to automatically generate diverse structures and buildings, mimicking the creative style of players or following specific architectural principles.
2. **Procedural Generation of Levels**:
   - **Procedural generation** refers to the use of algorithms to automatically create content based on predefined rules and randomness. AI can generate new **game levels**, **maps**, and **environments** by combining and modifying various

elements like terrain, obstacles, enemies, and puzzles.

- o AI can ensure that these generated levels are not only unique but also playable, balanced, and engaging. For example, a racing game might use AI to create dynamic race tracks, while a platformer could generate procedurally created levels with varying difficulties and challenges.

3. **AI-Driven Storytelling and Quest Generation**:
   - o Generative AI can be used to create dynamic stories and quests by analyzing large amounts of narrative data, character interactions, and branching dialogues. AI models can generate story arcs based on user preferences or player actions, allowing for adaptive narratives.
   - o **Natural language processing (NLP)** models like **GPT-3** can be used to generate **dialogues** and **interactive scripts** that react to player input, creating a more immersive and engaging experience where the storyline unfolds uniquely for each player.

4. **AI-Generated Music and Sound Effects**:
   - o AI can also assist with the creation of **dynamic music** and **sound effects** that evolve based on the player's progress and actions. By analyzing the gameplay, AI can generate music that complements the atmosphere of different in-game events, such as combat sequences or exploration.

Real-World Example: Procedural Generation in Video Games

Procedural generation is one of the most prominent applications of AI in game design. It is particularly useful in creating vast, dynamic game worlds that feel unique for each player. Let's explore a few examples of **procedural generation** in **video games**:

1. **No Man's Sky**:
    o **No Man's Sky** is a prime example of **procedural generation** in a game. The game allows players to explore an **entire universe** with over 18 quintillion planets, each with unique landscapes, ecosystems, and creatures. The game uses AI algorithms to generate planets, terrain, flora, fauna, weather systems, and even the game's narrative content.
    o Each planet in the game is procedurally generated based on algorithms that consider factors like the planet's size, its atmosphere, its gravity, and its potential for life. This vast universe would be impossible to manually create, but with AI-driven procedural generation, the game offers an enormous amount of content without requiring endless handcrafting by developers.
2. **Minecraft**:
    o **Minecraft** uses procedural generation to create the game's **worlds** and **biomes**.

The game's randomly generated landscapes include forests, oceans, deserts, and mountains, all of which are created using an algorithm based on seed values that control how the terrain and structures are arranged.

- The procedural generation in **Minecraft** ensures that every world is unique, and it offers endless possibilities for exploration and creativity. AI models can enhance this further by automatically generating buildings, dungeons, and other in-game features to add even more variety to the player experience.

3. **Spelunky**:
   - **Spelunky**, a roguelike platformer, utilizes procedural generation to create new **dungeons** and **levels** every time the player enters the game. The goal is to generate levels that are fun, challenging, and fair, with randomized obstacles, enemies, and loot.
   - The AI behind **Spelunky's** procedural generation ensures that levels remain balanced, with the difficulty scaling in a way that makes the game engaging. It achieves this by using algorithms that control the placement of items, traps, and enemies in a way that's challenging yet not overwhelmingly difficult.

4. **The Elder Scrolls II: Daggerfall**:
   - **Daggerfall**, the second installment in the Elder Scrolls series, is known for its

massive world, which spans over 15,000 cities, towns, and villages. The game uses procedural generation to create the world's vast landscapes, dungeons, and towns, making it one of the largest open-world games ever created.

o While the game's procedural generation doesn't achieve the same level of detail as later titles, it demonstrated the power of AI in generating vast, explorable worlds in a way that wouldn't have been possible with traditional manual design.

Summary

In this chapter, we explored how **generative AI** is transforming the field of **game design** by enabling the **procedural generation** of **game assets**, **levels**, and **stories**. AI is playing a pivotal role in reducing the time and effort involved in traditional game design, while simultaneously introducing new possibilities for creativity and gameplay.

We discussed how AI can generate realistic assets, dynamic game levels, and interactive storylines based on player actions and text descriptions. **Procedural generation**, in particular, has revolutionized the way vast game worlds and diverse content are created, allowing developers to build immersive, expansive environments without the need for excessive manual labor.

Real-world examples, like **No Man's Sky, Minecraft**, and **Spelunky**, demonstrate the practical applications of procedural generation in creating dynamic and engaging game worlds. As AI continues to evolve, we can expect even more sophisticated and personalized gaming experiences that adapt to the player's actions and preferences.

CHAPTER THIRTEEN

Ethical Implications of Generative AI

Addressing Bias and Fairness in AI-Generated Content

One of the most significant ethical challenges surrounding **Generative AI** is the presence of **bias** in the content it generates. Because AI models are trained on large datasets, they can inherit the biases that exist in those datasets, leading to the generation of content that is unfair, discriminatory, or reinforces stereotypes. This is especially concerning in applications such as content generation, recruitment, and decision-making, where AI has the potential to perpetuate harmful biases.

1. **Bias in Training Data**:
   o AI models learn patterns from the data they are trained on, and if the training data contains biases (whether explicit or implicit), the model will likely generate biased content. For example, if a generative AI is trained on text data that includes biased language or historical inequalities, the model might produce content that reflects those biases.
   o **Example**: A text-to-image model trained on data that disproportionately represents one race, gender, or culture may generate images that overrepresent certain demographics and underrepresent others,

reinforcing stereotypes or marginalizing certain groups.

2. **Fairness in Content Generation**:
   - Ensuring **fairness** in AI-generated content involves ensuring that the model generates content that is inclusive and representative of all groups, without perpetuating stereotypes or excluding certain perspectives. This includes fair representation in visual art, music, literature, and even the narratives generated by AI in storytelling.
   - **Steps to Mitigate Bias**:
     - **Diverse Datasets**: One way to reduce bias is to train AI models on diverse datasets that include a broad range of perspectives, cultures, and voices. This helps ensure that AI-generated content is more inclusive and representative.
     - **Bias Auditing**: Another approach is regularly auditing AI systems for bias, using specific metrics to identify whether the generated content disproportionately favors one group over another.
     - **Transparency and Accountability**: Developers must be transparent about how their models are trained, what data is used, and how content generation decisions are made. This ensures

that any inherent biases can be identified and corrected.

3. **Ensuring Ethical Standards**:
   o Ethical guidelines for generative AI models are crucial. These guidelines should promote fairness, transparency, and accountability. Efforts should be made to continuously evaluate and adjust AI systems as they evolve, ensuring that they don't perpetuate harmful biases or produce discriminatory content.

How AI Can Be Misused: Deepfakes, Misinformation, and Privacy Concerns

As generative AI becomes more advanced, it also becomes more susceptible to **misuse**, raising significant ethical concerns related to **deepfakes**, **misinformation**, and **privacy**.

1. **Deepfakes**:
   o **Deepfakes** are AI-generated media, usually video or audio, that manipulate real footage or sound to create highly realistic but fabricated content. Using generative AI models, people can create videos where someone says or does things they never actually did.
   o **Potential Harm**:
      ▪ **Personal Damage**: Deepfakes can be used to impersonate individuals for malicious purposes, such as

defamation, blackmail, or impersonation.

- **Political Manipulation**: Deepfakes have been used in political contexts to spread misinformation, create fake news stories, or make it seem as though politicians or public figures have said or done things that they haven't.
- **Trust Erosion**: The ability to create hyper-realistic, fabricated content undermines public trust in media, making it more difficult to distinguish between real and fake information.

2. **Misinformation and Fake News**:
   o Generative AI has made it easier than ever to produce and spread **misinformation**. AI models can be used to generate convincing articles, social media posts, or even entire websites that spread false or misleading information. This is especially concerning when AI is used to create **news articles** or **scientific reports** that seem credible but are entirely fabricated.
   o **Real-World Example**: The spread of **fake news** related to politics, health (e.g., COVID-19 misinformation), and elections has been exacerbated by AI-generated content, as it is often harder to distinguish between real and fake information.

3. **Privacy Concerns**:

- o As generative AI models become more powerful, there are growing concerns around **privacy** and **data protection**. Many generative AI systems, including deep learning models, are trained on vast datasets that might include sensitive or private data. If these models are not adequately secured, they could inadvertently generate or expose private information.

- o **Data Scraping**: Some generative AI systems are trained on publicly available data scraped from the internet, which may include personal information, conversations, or images that were not intended for public use. This raises questions about whether individuals' personal data is being used without consent.

- o **Generative Models and Consent**: When AI is used to create content that mimics individuals (e.g., generating voices or faces), it raises concerns about consent. Who owns the generated content, especially when it's based on someone's likeness or voice? This is a significant issue when it comes to **deepfakes** and AI-generated content featuring celebrities, influencers, or even private citizens.

Real-World Example: The Ethics of AI-Generated Art and Music

The use of generative AI in **art** and **music creation** presents several ethical questions related to **authorship**, **ownership**, and **creative expression**.

1. **Authorship and Ownership**:
   - **AI-generated art** raises questions about who owns the rights to a piece of art created by a machine. Is the artist who provided the input prompt the rightful owner, or is it the developer of the AI model? What if the AI model was trained using copyrighted artwork without permission from the original artists?
   - **Example**: Consider a scenario where an artist uses a text-to-image AI tool to generate a painting based on a prompt. The artist might then sell the painting for a profit. Who owns the rights to the painting? The artist who provided the prompt, the creator of the AI tool, or the creators of the dataset the model was trained on?
   - Similarly, AI-generated **music** raises the question of ownership: if a generative AI creates an original piece of music, who holds the copyright to the composition? Is it the developer who created the AI, the person who provided the initial input, or the AI itself?

2. **The Devaluation of Human Creativity**:

- Some critics argue that AI-generated art and music could **devalue** human creativity. As AI tools become more sophisticated, they can produce high-quality creative work in a fraction of the time it would take human artists. This raises concerns about the potential for AI to replace human creators in fields like graphic design, music composition, and illustration.
- On the other hand, proponents of AI in the arts argue that AI tools can empower artists by providing new ways to express their creativity and streamline their workflow. Instead of replacing human creativity, AI can be seen as a tool that complements and enhances artistic expression.

3. **Cultural Appropriation**:
- There are also concerns about **cultural appropriation** in AI-generated art and music. When AI is trained on vast datasets that include cultural artifacts, styles, and genres from around the world, there is a risk that it may appropriate elements of marginalized cultures without proper context or respect for their origins. This could lead to a homogenization of art, where unique cultural identities are diluted or misrepresented.

4. **Ethical AI Use in the Arts**:
- To address these ethical concerns, it's essential that developers and users of

generative AI tools consider the impact of their work on human artists and cultural communities. This involves ensuring that AI-generated content is used responsibly and that proper **credit and compensation** are given to the original creators whose work contributed to the AI's training data.

Summary

In this chapter, we explored the **ethical implications** of generative AI, particularly concerning **bias, misuse,** and **ownership**. As AI models become more capable of generating art, music, and video, it's crucial to address the potential risks and challenges they pose. Ensuring **fairness** and **accountability** in AI-generated content requires thoughtful consideration of the data used to train models, the potential for misuse in creating **deepfakes** or **misinformation**, and the ethical questions surrounding **ownership** and **authorship** in creative works.

As generative AI continues to evolve, it will be essential to strike a balance between innovation and ethical responsibility. By creating frameworks that address these concerns, we can ensure that AI serves as a tool for enhancing creativity, rather than undermining it.

CHAPTER FOURTEEN

Intellectual Property and Copyright in the Age of AI

Who Owns AI-Generated Content?

The question of **ownership** regarding AI-generated content has become a critical issue as generative AI continues to play a more prominent role in content creation across various industries, including **art**, **music**, **literature**, and **software development**. Traditionally, copyright law has recognized human creators as the rightful owners of their works, granting them the exclusive rights to reproduce, distribute, and display their creations. However, with AI taking on more creative roles, the issue of ownership has become more complex.

1. **AI as a Tool or Creator?**:
    o In traditional creative processes, the **creator** is typically a person—an artist, writer, musician, or filmmaker. When AI is involved, however, the line between human and machine creativity becomes blurred. AI tools are often used by individuals to generate content, but the degree of human involvement varies. In some cases, the human creator provides an input or prompt, and the AI produces a result based on that prompt. In other cases, the AI may operate autonomously,

generating content with minimal human input.

- o This raises the fundamental question: **Who owns the content generated by AI?** Should it be the person who provided the prompt or input, the developer of the AI tool, or the AI system itself?

2. **The Role of AI Developers**:
   - o One perspective is that **AI developers** who create the underlying models and algorithms should hold the intellectual property rights to the content generated by their tools. After all, the AI's creativity is based on the architecture and training that the developers have built.
   - o However, if AI-generated content is viewed as a collaborative effort between the human user and the AI system, the **user** (who provides the prompt and directs the process) may be entitled to claim ownership of the final product. This scenario is common in many AI-driven platforms, where users are granted licenses or full ownership of the content they create with the AI.

3. **Legal Precedents and Copyright Law**:
   - o In many countries, copyright law does not explicitly account for **AI-generated works,** as the law has traditionally been designed to protect human-created content. The U.S. Copyright Office, for example, has stated that works created by non-human entities, such as AI, cannot be

granted copyright protection. This means that unless a human author is involved in the creation process, the AI-generated content may not be eligible for copyright protection.

○ In contrast, some legal experts argue that **AI should be treated as a co-creator**, with human users retaining the rights to the content they guide or influence. This could allow for greater flexibility in granting copyright protection while ensuring that the rights of both the AI developers and human users are recognized.

Understanding Copyright in the Context of Generative AI

Copyright law was originally designed to protect the rights of creators, ensuring they have control over their works and can monetize them. However, in the context of generative AI, traditional definitions of authorship and ownership are being challenged.

1. **Who Can Claim Copyright?**:
   ○ Copyright traditionally requires a **human author**. In the case of AI, there is no human author directly creating the content in the traditional sense. This creates ambiguity, especially when it comes to **works that are autonomously generated** by AI systems with minimal or no human intervention.

- o For example, if an AI generates a painting from a text prompt, does the human who provided the prompt have the rights to the painting? Or does the AI developer, who created the underlying algorithms, own the rights? These questions are difficult to answer under current copyright frameworks, which do not foresee AI as a potential creator.

2. **Derivative Works**:
   - o AI systems, especially those used for **art generation** or **music creation**, are often trained on vast datasets that include pre-existing works. This raises the issue of whether AI-generated content constitutes a **derivative work** of the content it was trained on. For example, if an AI is trained on a large set of paintings and then creates a new image, is the AI creating something that is too similar to the works it was trained on, thereby violating the copyrights of the original artists?
   - o The **fair use** doctrine may come into play in some cases, allowing the use of copyrighted works for purposes such as research, education, or commentary. However, the line between **fair use** and **infringement** becomes blurred when AI is involved, as AI models may create works that are too similar to their training data, even if the generated content is unique in some ways.

3. **Licensing and Ownership**:

- o Many platforms that offer AI tools for content creation (such as AI-generated art or music) provide users with **licenses** to the content they generate. These licenses vary in terms of usage rights, with some platforms allowing users to retain full ownership of the content, while others retain some form of control over how the generated content can be used, distributed, or commercialized.
- o **AI-generated content licenses** are still evolving, and legal frameworks will likely continue to adjust to better accommodate the unique nature of AI content creation. Some experts argue that a new class of **AI-specific intellectual property laws** may eventually emerge to address these issues.

Real-World Example: Legal Challenges in AI Art Ownership

As generative AI becomes increasingly capable of creating **art** and other creative works, several high-profile legal challenges have emerged regarding ownership and copyright. One notable case involved **AI-generated art** and the legal battle over who owns the rights to the artwork created by an AI system.

1. **The "Edmond de Belamy" Case**:
   - o In 2018, an AI-generated portrait titled **"Portrait of Edmond de Belamy"** was

sold at **Christie's Auction House** for over \$432,000. The portrait was created by an AI system called **Obvious**, which was trained on a dataset of portraits by European masters. The portrait depicted a blurry, surreal figure, and the auction sale prompted a legal and philosophical debate about the ownership of AI-generated art.

o The creators of the portrait, a French collective known as **Obvious**, stated that they provided the input prompts and directed the AI in creating the portrait, claiming ownership of the work. However, many questioned whether the creators of the AI model (the developers) should have a stake in the ownership.

o **Christie's Auction House** explicitly stated that the work was **AI-generated**, but the issue of copyright remained ambiguous. The controversy highlighted the ongoing legal and ethical concerns about who holds the rights to AI-generated art—whether it's the AI developers, the users who provide input, or the AI itself.

2. **The "AI Music Composition" Case**:

o Another example is the case of **AI-generated music**. AI tools such as **Amper Music** and **AIVA** have enabled non-musicians to create original tracks by simply selecting parameters like mood, genre, and instruments. This has led to a debate about who owns the rights to music composed by AI.

- o In one case, a music composer used an AI tool to create a composition that was later sold as original music. The composer claimed ownership of the track, citing their creative direction in selecting the input parameters for the AI. However, the tool's developers argued that they retained some degree of ownership due to their role in creating the AI system that enabled the music generation.
- o These cases underscore the complexity of assigning authorship and ownership in a world where AI systems play an increasingly prominent role in content creation.

Summary

In this chapter, we delved into the complexities of **intellectual property (IP)** and **copyright** in the age of generative AI. The emergence of AI-generated content has raised important questions about ownership and authorship, as well as how traditional copyright laws should apply to non-human creators.

We explored the challenges around **AI ownership**, the **role of developers** in content creation, and the potential for AI systems to generate **derivative works** from pre-existing content. The discussion also highlighted how legal frameworks are struggling to keep up with the rapid evolution of AI in creative industries, with examples like the **AI-generated portrait** of Edmond de Belamy and the challenges surrounding **AI-generated music** ownership.

As AI continues to play an increasingly significant role in creative industries, establishing clearer **legal guidelines** and ethical standards will be essential to ensure that all parties—AI developers, users, and original creators—are fairly compensated and recognized for their contributions to the creative process.

CHAPTER FIFTEEN

AI in Healthcare: Generating Solutions for Medicine

How Generative AI is Transforming Healthcare and Drug Discovery

Generative AI has begun to make significant strides in **healthcare,** offering innovative solutions in a variety of areas such as **drug discovery, personalized medicine, medical imaging,** and **patient care.** These AI models are capable of analyzing vast amounts of medical data to generate insights, predictions, and even potential treatments. As the field continues to evolve, generative AI has the potential to reduce the time and cost involved in developing new treatments, improve diagnostic accuracy, and provide more targeted therapies for patients.

1. **AI in Drug Discovery**:
   - The process of **drug discovery** traditionally involves years of research and testing to identify compounds that could potentially become new medicines. Generative AI is revolutionizing this process by rapidly generating new molecular structures and predicting their potential effectiveness.
   - **Generative models** like **DeepMind's AlphaFold** have been used to predict the **3D structures of proteins**, providing

critical insights into disease mechanisms and accelerating drug development. AI can analyze existing medical literature and datasets to identify novel drug candidates or redesign existing compounds for better efficacy or fewer side effects.

o Additionally, AI can **optimize** drug formulations, predict interactions between different substances, and simulate clinical trials, reducing the need for costly and time-consuming experimentation.

2. **Personalized Medicine**:

o **Personalized medicine** is an emerging field where treatments are tailored to individual patients based on their genetic makeup, lifestyle, and other unique factors. Generative AI models can analyze patient data (e.g., genetic sequences, medical histories, and treatment responses) to recommend personalized treatment plans.

o For example, AI could generate targeted therapies for specific genetic mutations in cancer patients or predict how a patient might respond to a certain medication. This level of customization ensures better outcomes and minimizes adverse effects from ineffective treatments.

3. **AI-Driven Simulation and Modeling**:

o In addition to generating molecular structures, generative AI is also being used for **simulation** and **modeling** of biological systems. By creating digital twins of organs or entire body systems, AI can simulate how diseases develop, predict how a drug will interact with cells, and test various treatment strategies before they are implemented in clinical settings.

o AI models also allow researchers to simulate patient-specific disease progression, which can help in making more accurate predictions regarding the outcomes of treatment regimens.

Generating Medical Imaging and Diagnostics with AI

Generative AI has become a crucial tool in **medical imaging** and diagnostics, enabling faster, more accurate, and more detailed analyses of medical images like X-rays, CT scans, MRIs, and ultrasounds. By combining **computer vision** techniques with generative modeling, AI can assist healthcare professionals in identifying patterns and anomalies that might otherwise be overlooked.

1. **Medical Image Generation and Enhancement**:

o **Generative models** are used to enhance or generate synthetic medical images, which can be particularly useful in situations where high-quality data is limited. For instance, AI can generate missing slices of CT or MRI scans to create complete images or improve the resolution of medical images for clearer analysis.

- **Example**: AI-driven tools like **GANs (Generative Adversarial Networks)** can generate high-resolution images from low-quality scans, providing doctors with better visuals for diagnosis and treatment planning. This could significantly improve imaging technologies, particularly in under-resourced healthcare settings where high-quality medical imaging equipment may not be available.

2. **Improving Diagnosis with AI-Enhanced Imaging**:
   - Generative AI models can also be used to help **diagnose diseases** by analyzing medical images. These AI models are trained to recognize patterns and anomalies in images, such as tumors, fractures, or other pathologies, with a level of accuracy that rivals or even exceeds human experts.
   - AI tools can automatically detect and highlight areas of concern in medical scans, allowing healthcare professionals to focus their attention on the most critical aspects of a patient's health. This reduces the risk of human error and improves diagnostic speed and accuracy.
   - **AI-Assisted Diagnosis**: For example, a deep learning model trained on a vast

dataset of radiology images can detect early signs of diseases like **cancer, pneumonia,** or **cardiovascular conditions,** providing a second opinion or acting as a diagnostic tool for healthcare professionals.

3. **AI in Pathology**:
   o Pathologists can use AI-driven tools to analyze biopsy slides and tissue samples. AI can generate synthetic pathological images or identify anomalies, such as **cancerous cells** or **infected tissues,** within microscope slides. These tools help pathologists make faster and more accurate diagnoses, reducing the time required to provide results and improving patient outcomes.

Real-World Example: AI in Cancer Detection and Treatment Design

Cancer diagnosis and treatment design are among the most critical applications of AI in healthcare. Early detection and personalized treatment are key to improving survival rates, and AI has the potential to dramatically enhance both areas.

1. **AI in Cancer Detection**:
   o AI systems are already being used in clinical settings to assist doctors in detecting **cancerous lesions, tumors,** and **abnormal growths**. Generative AI

models trained on vast datasets of **medical images** (including mammograms, CT scans, and biopsies) can identify cancer at early stages, even before human doctors can spot it.

- o **Example**: One of the most notable applications is the use of **AI models for breast cancer detection** in mammograms. AI tools can analyze mammogram images and generate an output indicating the probability of cancerous tissue. These models are designed to help radiologists identify areas that require further examination or biopsy, potentially saving lives by identifying early-stage cancers that might otherwise go undetected.

2. **Personalized Treatment Design**:
   - o Beyond detection, AI is also helping to design **personalized cancer treatments**. By analyzing a patient's genetic data and tumor characteristics, AI can help design targeted therapies that are most likely to work for that particular patient, reducing the need for trial-and-error treatment approaches.
   - o **Generative AI in Chemotherapy Design**: For example, AI systems can generate new combinations of **chemotherapy drugs** that are tailored to a patient's genetic profile, maximizing the effectiveness of treatment while minimizing side effects. AI models can

also predict the likelihood of treatment success or failure, allowing doctors to adjust treatment plans accordingly.

3. **AI-Assisted Radiotherapy Planning**:
   - AI-driven models are also being used to optimize **radiotherapy** treatments. Radiotherapy requires precise targeting of cancerous cells while avoiding damage to healthy tissue. Generative AI can help design treatment plans that ensure radiation is directed with the highest possible precision, improving outcomes and reducing side effects.

4. **Drug Discovery for Cancer**:
   - In drug discovery, AI is helping researchers design **novel cancer drugs** by generating molecular compounds that could target specific genetic mutations or tumor types. These AI systems analyze existing drug candidates, study their effectiveness, and generate new compounds that could be more effective in treating specific types of cancer.
   - **Example**: The development of **targeted therapies** for cancers like lung cancer or breast cancer has been accelerated through the use of AI models, which simulate how different compounds might interact with cancer cells and predict their potential to halt cancer growth.

Summary

In this chapter, we explored the transformative impact of **Generative AI in healthcare**, particularly in areas like **drug discovery**, **medical imaging**, and **personalized treatment**. AI models are being used to generate solutions for complex problems in medicine, accelerating the development of treatments, improving diagnostic accuracy, and personalizing therapies for individual patients.

We discussed how AI is helping to revolutionize **cancer detection**, generating highly accurate **medical images** for diagnosis, and even designing **personalized treatment plans**. Real-world examples, such as AI-driven tools for detecting early-stage cancer and optimizing radiotherapy treatments, demonstrate the power of AI in improving patient outcomes.

As AI continues to evolve, its potential to reshape healthcare is immense, providing faster, more efficient, and more personalized solutions that will benefit patients worldwide.

CHAPTER SIXTEEN

AI-Powered Writing Tools and Content Creation

How GPT Models are Used for Content Creation and Copywriting

Generative Pretrained Transformer (GPT) models, such as **GPT-3** and **GPT-4**, have become increasingly popular in the field of content creation and **copywriting**. These AI models are capable of producing high-quality written content based on textual prompts, making them valuable tools for writers, marketers, and content creators across a variety of industries.

1. **Content Generation**:
   o GPT models are trained on vast datasets of text and have a deep understanding of **grammar**, **syntax**, and **context**. They can generate **articles**, **blog posts**, **product descriptions**, **advertisements**, and even **novels** in a matter of seconds, significantly reducing the time and effort required for content creation.
   o By providing a brief prompt or idea, GPT can generate coherent, well-structured content in the desired style and tone. This is particularly useful for **copywriters**, who often need to produce high volumes of content quickly and efficiently.

2. **Copywriting**:
   - **Copywriting** is one of the most common applications of GPT models in content creation. GPT can be used to generate **ad copy**, **email campaigns**, and **landing page content**, helping businesses craft persuasive messaging to engage customers and drive conversions.
   - **Personalization**: GPT models can also generate personalized copy, tailored to different audience segments, by analyzing customer data and preferences. This allows marketers to create content that resonates with their target audience, improving customer engagement and sales.
3. **Content Ideation and Drafting**:
   - Writers often face the challenge of **content ideation**—coming up with new and engaging topics. GPT models can assist with brainstorming by generating topic suggestions, headlines, or outlines based on a keyword or subject matter.
   - Once a topic is selected, GPT can help with the **drafting process** by generating a first draft or expanding on an idea, giving writers a solid starting point from which they can refine the content and add their own voice.

The Role of AI in Blogging, News, and Social Media

AI-powered writing tools, particularly GPT models, are reshaping the landscape of **blogging**, **news**, and **social media** content creation. These tools have become an essential part of the content creation process for both large media organizations and individual content creators.

1. **AI in Blogging**:
    o **Automated Blogging**: Many bloggers use GPT-powered tools to streamline the process of creating regular blog posts. By providing a brief topic or keyword, AI can generate a full-length article, saving time and effort. Bloggers can then refine the generated content to match their tone and style.
    o **SEO Optimization**: AI can also assist in **search engine optimization (SEO)** by generating content that incorporates relevant keywords and follows SEO best practices. This ensures that blog posts are more likely to rank highly on search engines, driving organic traffic to websites.
    o **Consistency**: For content creators who need to produce blog posts frequently, AI can ensure a consistent flow of content. With AI-generated articles, bloggers can maintain an active posting schedule without compromising quality.
2. **AI in News**:

- o **Automated Journalism**: GPT models are increasingly being used by news organizations to generate automated reports on topics like finance, sports, and weather. These AI systems are trained to gather information from reliable sources and generate news articles in real time.
- o **Breaking News**: AI tools can generate **breaking news updates** based on available information, providing a fast response to current events. For example, an AI model might generate an article summarizing the key points of a press release or official statement as soon as it becomes available, allowing news outlets to stay on top of emerging stories.
- o **Personalized News**: AI can also curate personalized news content based on user preferences, ensuring that readers receive articles on topics that interest them. This enhances user engagement and keeps audiences returning to news platforms.

3. **AI in Social Media**:
   - o **Content Creation**: GPT-powered tools are widely used to generate **social media posts** for platforms like Twitter, Facebook, Instagram, and LinkedIn. By providing a simple prompt or keyword, marketers can generate engaging posts tailored to the specific requirements of each platform.
   - o **Social Media Campaigns**: AI can also be used to create **social media campaigns**,

including writing captions, creating hashtags, and generating ad copy. This helps businesses maintain an active and consistent social media presence while reducing the time and effort spent on content creation.

o **Engagement**: AI can assist in engaging with followers by generating responses to comments or direct messages. By analyzing previous conversations and interactions, AI can generate personalized replies that mimic human interaction, improving customer service and community engagement.

Real-World Example: Using AI to Write Articles and Social Media Posts

Let's explore a real-world example of how AI-powered writing tools are being used to generate **articles** and **social media posts**:

1. **AI in Newsrooms**:
   o **The Associated Press** and **Reuters** have used AI to automate the creation of financial reports and sports news articles. For instance, The Associated Press uses AI to generate earnings reports for thousands of companies each quarter. These reports are based on a set of structured data (such as financial results), which the AI analyzes and turns into

readable content that can be quickly published.

- o Similarly, AI is used to generate sports coverage, such as game summaries and player statistics. The AI processes the game data, generates the key points, and drafts the article within minutes, allowing journalists to focus on more complex tasks like feature writing and investigative reporting.

2. **AI in Blogging and Content Marketing**:
   - o **Content marketing agencies** often use AI writing tools like **Jarvis (now Jasper)** or **Writesonic** to generate blog posts, product descriptions, and marketing emails. These tools help marketers save time by automating content creation, while still ensuring the output is relevant, SEO-optimized, and aligned with the brand's voice.
   - o For example, an e-commerce website might use AI to generate descriptions for thousands of products. The AI model can generate unique, high-quality descriptions that highlight key features and benefits, ensuring that each product page is optimized for search engines.

3. **AI in Social Media Content**:
   - o Social media management platforms like **Buffer** and **Hootsuite** integrate AI-powered tools to help users create social media posts. For example, **Copy.ai** and **Writesonic** are tools that marketers use to

generate catchy headlines, engaging posts, and attention-grabbing captions for Instagram or Twitter based on a given topic or brand identity.

- o A real-world example is **AI-generated marketing campaigns** for product launches. A company launching a new product might use AI tools to generate a series of posts across multiple platforms, adapting the content to the tone and format best suited to each platform (e.g., shorter, punchier posts for Twitter, more detailed ones for Facebook or LinkedIn).

Summary

In this chapter, we explored the growing impact of **AI-powered writing tools** in the world of **content creation**, including their role in **blogging, news, social media**, and **copywriting**. GPT models, such as **GPT-3** and **GPT-4**, have revolutionized the way content is generated, making it faster, more efficient, and more accessible for businesses and individuals alike.

We discussed how AI tools are being used to generate high-quality articles, product descriptions, social media posts, and marketing copy, helping marketers and creators produce content at scale without sacrificing quality. Real-world examples, like AI-generated news articles, automated blog posts, and social media campaigns, demonstrate how AI is reshaping the landscape of content creation across industries.

As these tools continue to evolve, their potential to streamline the content creation process will only grow, empowering businesses and individuals to reach new audiences and engage more effectively with their followers.

CHAPTER SEVEN

AI for Personalization and Recommendation Systems

How AI Personalizes User Experiences

Personalization is one of the most powerful applications of **artificial intelligence** (AI) today. By analyzing user data and understanding individual preferences, AI can create highly customized experiences across a range of industries, from **e-commerce** and **entertainment** to **social media** and **online education**. The goal of AI-driven personalization is to make interactions more relevant, engaging, and efficient for users, ultimately improving user satisfaction, increasing engagement, and driving conversions.

1. **User Data and Behavior Analysis**:
   o AI personalizes experiences by analyzing vast amounts of **user data**, including browsing history, search patterns, purchase history, and social media interactions. By identifying patterns and preferences, AI can predict what a user is likely to be interested in next and present that information in a tailored way.
   o **Machine learning (ML) algorithms** are particularly useful in this context, as they can continuously learn from user

interactions and adjust recommendations in real-time. Over time, the system becomes more accurate at predicting and personalizing content for each individual user.

2. **User Segmentation**:
   - o AI also uses **user segmentation** techniques to group users with similar interests or behaviors, allowing platforms to deliver more precise recommendations. For example, a streaming service might identify that users who watch a particular genre of movies are more likely to enjoy a specific type of TV show, and will tailor recommendations accordingly.
   - o This type of segmentation can also be applied to **marketing**, where AI-driven tools can deliver personalized ads to different customer segments based on their behaviors and demographics.

3. **Dynamic Personalization**:
   - o **Dynamic personalization** refers to how AI systems can adapt and adjust content or recommendations in real-time based on changes in user behavior. For instance, if a user shifts their preferences—such as suddenly showing interest in a new genre of music, or opting for different products—AI models can quickly adjust their recommendations to match these new preferences.
   - o This dynamic approach ensures that users are always presented with fresh, relevant

content that suits their evolving needs and desires.

Generative AI, which includes models like **GPT**, **GANs (Generative Adversarial Networks)**, and **variational autoencoders (VAEs)**, plays a key role in enhancing **recommender systems** by generating personalized content or product suggestions that align with users' preferences.

1. **Content Generation and Personalization**:
   o **Generative models** can create personalized recommendations not only by analyzing past behavior but also by generating **new content** based on that information. For example, in **e-commerce**, AI might generate personalized product descriptions or advertisements tailored to a user's preferences.
   o In music or movie recommendation systems, generative AI can go beyond simply recommending similar content based on past behavior. It can **create unique content** or suggest new, innovative combinations of genres, artists, or movie themes, increasing the diversity of recommendations while still matching the user's tastes.
2. **Hybrid Approaches**:

- Many modern recommender systems use **hybrid models,** combining both **content-based** and **collaborative filtering** approaches with generative techniques. For example, content-based filtering uses attributes of items (like genres or descriptions), while collaborative filtering focuses on user behavior, finding patterns between users and items. Generative AI can then be added to provide more diverse and tailored suggestions, enriching the recommendation process.
- A hybrid model might combine the personalization of **collaborative filtering** (suggesting items based on similar users) with the **creativity** of generative AI (suggesting entirely new types of products or content based on user interests).

3. **Dynamic and Contextual Recommendations**:
   - Generative AI models are adept at considering **context**—such as the time of day, location, and current mood—to provide **dynamic recommendations**. For example, a movie recommendation system might suggest light-hearted films during the day, while recommending more intense thrillers in the evening when the user has more time to watch.
   - Similarly, an AI model used for music streaming could suggest more relaxing

tunes during work hours and more energetic tracks when a user is exercising.

Real-World Example: AI Recommendations on Platforms like Netflix, Amazon, and Spotify

AI-driven recommendation systems are used extensively by major platforms like **Netflix**, **Amazon**, and **Spotify** to personalize user experiences and provide content that aligns with individual preferences. Here's how AI plays a role on each of these platforms:

1. **Netflix**:
    o   **Netflix** uses AI to personalize movie and TV show recommendations based on viewing history, search behavior, and user ratings. By analyzing these data points, Netflix can predict what content a user is likely to enjoy.
    o   One of the key techniques used by Netflix is **collaborative filtering**, which involves identifying users with similar preferences and recommending shows that others in the same group have watched and enjoyed.
    o   Additionally, Netflix uses **content-based filtering** by analyzing the characteristics of shows (e.g., genre, actors, themes) to suggest similar titles. **Deep learning algorithms** are employed to fine-tune these recommendations and make them more dynamic and accurate over time.

- o **Generative AI** plays a role in content creation as well—such as generating personalized promotional trailers or suggesting personalized storylines for interactive content like *Bandersnatch*.

2. **Amazon**:
   - o **Amazon** uses AI to recommend products based on user behavior, search history, and purchase patterns. The platform combines both **collaborative filtering** (suggesting products based on other customers' similar purchases) and **content-based filtering** (suggesting items with similar attributes to those the user has bought or browsed).
   - o Additionally, Amazon uses **generative AI** to suggest **bundled products** or **complementary items** that a customer might be interested in based on their past purchases. For example, if a user buys a camera, Amazon might recommend camera accessories or lenses, often in creative combinations that the user has not explicitly searched for.

3. **Spotify**:
   - o **Spotify** uses **AI-based recommendation algorithms** to personalize music playlists, radio stations, and recommendations for each user. The platform analyzes listening behavior (e.g., genre preferences, favorite artists, and song characteristics like tempo and mood)

to create tailored playlists such as *Discover Weekly* and *Release Radar.*

o **Generative AI** plays a role in music suggestions by creating dynamic playlists that combine user preferences with new and evolving trends in music, making the recommendations both personal and fresh. For example, Spotify might suggest an artist similar to a user's favorite, but with a **generative twist**, recommending lesser-known tracks or emerging artists with a similar style.

o Spotify also uses **natural language processing (NLP)** to analyze user-generated content, such as song reviews and lyrics, to further refine its recommendations and improve accuracy.

Summary

In this chapter, we explored how **AI-powered personalization** and **recommendation systems** are transforming user experiences across various platforms, including **Netflix**, **Amazon**, and **Spotify**. By leveraging AI, these platforms can analyze user behavior, preferences, and past interactions to deliver highly tailored content—whether it's movies, products, or music.

We also discussed how **generative AI** is playing a key role in enriching the recommendation process, creating more diverse, dynamic, and relevant suggestions by considering not just past behaviors, but also user context, preferences, and the exploration of new content.

AI-powered recommendation systems are not only enhancing personalization but also reshaping industries by making interactions more engaging, relevant, and customized to individual tastes, thus improving overall user satisfaction and engagement.

CHAPTER EIGHTEEN

The Intersection of Generative AI and Virtual Reality

Combining AI with Virtual and Augmented Reality

The intersection of **Generative AI**, **Virtual Reality (VR)**, and **Augmented Reality (AR)** represents one of the most exciting frontiers in technology. Both VR and AR aim to immerse users in digital environments, while AI enhances these experiences by generating dynamic, interactive, and responsive content. By combining these technologies, creators can build entirely new worlds, interactive narratives, and realistic environments that adapt in real-time to user interactions.

1. **Virtual Reality (VR):**
    o **VR** immerses users in fully digital, computer-generated environments. Unlike traditional computer interfaces, VR allows users to interact with 3D spaces in a way that mimics the real world. VR requires specialized hardware, including headsets (like Oculus Rift, HTC Vive, or PlayStation VR) and sometimes additional accessories like motion controllers or haptic feedback devices.
    o AI plays a crucial role in **VR** by enhancing the realism of the experience

and making virtual environments more interactive. AI models can control in-game behaviors, such as how virtual characters react to the user's actions, how the environment evolves, and how the storyline adapts to player choices.

2. **Augmented Reality (AR)**:
    o   **AR**, on the other hand, overlays digital elements on top of the real world, typically through smartphones, tablets, or AR glasses (like Microsoft HoloLens or Google Glass). In AR, the user sees both their physical surroundings and virtual elements, which are integrated into their view in real-time.
    o   AI is used to create **context-aware experiences** in AR. For example, AI can recognize objects in the real world, and based on that recognition, it can project relevant information or interactive digital content. AI's ability to analyze and interpret real-world scenes is essential for **augmented reality's adaptability**.

3. **AI as the Key Enabler**:
    o   AI is the driving force behind **smart, adaptive VR and AR environments**. It can personalize experiences based on user behavior, track movements and gestures, create virtual entities that respond to users, and even generate new content in real-time. The goal is to make virtual experiences feel as interactive and engaging as the real world, offering a

seamless integration of physical and digital experiences.

How AI Generates Immersive Environments and Experiences

Generative AI is transforming VR and AR by providing tools to **automatically create dynamic, immersive environments** that adapt to users' actions, preferences, and contexts. AI's ability to generate content quickly and creatively can lead to rich, evolving experiences that feel alive and responsive.

1. **Creating Dynamic VR Worlds**:
    o One of the most exciting applications of AI in VR is the generation of **dynamic, procedurally generated worlds**. Rather than pre-building static environments, AI can generate unique landscapes, cities, or even entire planets based on user input or randomization.
    o **Example**: In an exploration-based VR game, AI can continuously generate new terrain as the player progresses, ensuring that no two playthroughs are the same. From forests to mountains to underground caves, AI can create complex environments that respond to the player's exploration, making every journey feel unique.
2. **Adaptive Virtual Characters**:

- o AI also plays a pivotal role in creating **intelligent NPCs (non-playable characters)** within VR. These characters can respond to player actions in **real-time**, interact with the environment, and even exhibit emotions or make decisions based on the player's behavior. This level of interaction brings a sense of **life** to virtual worlds.
- o In VR simulations or games, characters can have **conversations** with players, making dialogue trees less linear and more fluid. For example, in a VR role-playing game (RPG), the NPCs may learn from the player's previous choices and adapt their behavior, creating a highly personalized experience.

3. **Procedural Animation and Real-Time Content Generation**:
   - o Generative AI also enhances VR experiences by generating **real-time animations** for characters, objects, and the environment. As a user moves through a VR world, AI can generate animations that reflect how objects interact with one another, how physics behaves, and how characters move through the space.
   - o This is particularly useful in VR simulations, where the environment needs to react to the user's actions in real-time. For example, when a user picks up an object in a VR space, AI models can generate the appropriate animation for the

object's interaction, like how it fits in the user's hand, how it moves, and how it reacts to external forces.

4. **Creating Immersive Audio**:
   o AI can also be used to generate **immersive audio** that enhances the realism of VR and AR experiences. By analyzing the virtual environment, AI models can create dynamic soundscapes that change based on the user's location or actions. For example, in a VR forest, the AI might generate the sound of wind rustling through the trees, birds singing in the distance, or the crunch of footsteps on the ground.
   o In AR, AI can help position sounds spatially, ensuring that sounds feel anchored to real-world objects, adding to the sense of immersion.

Real-World Example: Virtual Reality Art and AI-Generated Worlds

The combination of **Generative AI** and **Virtual Reality** has opened up exciting new possibilities for artists and creators to generate fully immersive, interactive worlds that feel alive and dynamic. One of the most notable applications of this intersection is in **VR art** and **AI-generated worlds**.

1. **AI in Virtual Reality Art**:

- o **VR art** has become a growing field, where artists use virtual reality tools to create immersive art installations, sculptures, and experiences. With the addition of generative AI, artists can now create not only static VR art but also interactive, evolving environments.
- o One such example is **Google Tilt Brush**, a VR painting tool that allows artists to paint in 3D space. When combined with AI, it can generate dynamic elements like animated textures, evolving color schemes, or AI-generated characters that interact with the artist's creations in real-time.
- o AI can also **generate procedural art** within VR environments. For instance, a virtual landscape could be procedurally generated by AI, with terrain, lighting, and objects changing in response to the artist's input or environmental factors, creating an ever-changing, interactive art piece.

2. **AI-Generated Virtual Worlds**:
   - o In **game development**, AI-powered systems are used to generate entire virtual worlds in **real-time**, creating immersive, interactive environments that evolve as users explore them. A good example is **No Man's Sky**, where the game's universe is procedurally generated by algorithms, creating a seemingly infinite number of

planets with unique landscapes, creatures, and ecosystems.

- o Another example is the use of **AI in architectural design** within VR. AI can generate realistic **3D models of buildings** and **interiors**, which can then be explored in virtual space. AI systems can adapt the designs based on user input, generating variations of floor plans, architectural styles, and layouts.
- o In **interactive storytelling**, AI can adapt the narrative of a VR experience based on how the user interacts with the environment. The AI can create branching storylines, adjust the difficulty level, or change the environment to reflect the user's decisions, creating an experience that feels truly dynamic.

3. **AI for VR in Education and Training**:
- o One of the most practical applications of AI and VR is in **education and training**. AI-generated VR environments can simulate complex scenarios—whether it's a surgical operation, a flight simulation, or a complex mechanical system—where the user can practice and learn without risk.
- o For example, in medical training, AI could generate virtual **anatomical models** that respond to user interactions in real-time, such as practicing surgery or diagnosing a virtual patient. The AI can adapt the scenario based on the trainee's

actions, creating a more personalized and immersive training experience.

Summary

In this chapter, we explored the **intersection of Generative AI and Virtual Reality (VR)**, examining how these technologies combine to create immersive, dynamic, and interactive experiences. AI enhances VR and **Augmented Reality (AR)** environments by generating content in real-time, adapting to user behavior, and creating responsive, personalized experiences. From **AI-generated worlds** and **art** to **immersive training simulations**, the integration of AI into VR and AR is transforming how we interact with virtual spaces.

We also highlighted real-world examples, including **AI in VR art, procedural world generation in gaming**, and the use of AI for creating **dynamic VR experiences** in industries like healthcare and education. The possibilities are vast, and as these technologies continue to evolve, the line between the physical and virtual worlds will become increasingly blurred, offering new opportunities for creators and users alike.

CHAPTER NINETEEN

Training Generative AI Models: A Step-by-Step Guide

The Basics of Model Training: Data Preparation, Architecture, and Optimization

Training **Generative AI** models involves a series of steps that allow the model to learn from large datasets and generate new content. The process requires careful planning and consideration of several factors, including **data preparation**, **model architecture**, and **optimization**. In this section, we'll break down these core concepts and explore how they contribute to training successful generative models.

1. **Data Preparation**:
    - **Data is the foundation** of any machine learning model, and generative AI models are no exception. To train a generative model, you need a large and diverse dataset that the model can learn from.
    - For text-based models like **GPT** (Generative Pretrained Transformer), the dataset typically consists of **text data**, such as books, articles, or web pages. For **image-based models** like **GANs (Generative Adversarial Networks)** or **Diffusion models**, the dataset consists of images or other forms of visual data.

o Data must be **preprocessed** before being fed into the model. This can involve tasks like:

- **Cleaning**: Removing irrelevant or noisy data that could affect the model's learning.
- **Tokenization**: In text models, tokenizing text into smaller units, such as words or subwords, so the model can process it efficiently.
- **Normalization**: In image models, normalizing pixel values to scale images to a consistent range, which helps the model learn effectively.
- **Augmentation**: For image-based models, data augmentation techniques like **rotation**, **scaling**, and **flipping** can be used to create variations in the training data, making the model more robust.

2. **Architecture**:

o The **architecture** of the generative AI model defines how the model processes data and generates new outputs. Different generative models have different architectures based on their goals and the type of content they generate.

- **GPT** models use a **transformer architecture**, which relies on **self-attention mechanisms** to process long sequences of text and understand context across the entire input.

- **GANs** consist of two neural networks: a **generator** that creates content and a **discriminator** that evaluates it. These two networks are trained together in an adversarial setting, where the generator aims to fool the discriminator into thinking the generated content is real.

- **Diffusion models** (like Stable Diffusion) use a different approach by gradually adding noise to data and then reversing the process to generate new content. This process involves complex mathematical operations to generate high-quality images from noise or other starting points.

3. **Optimization**:
   - Once the data and architecture are ready, the model must be **trained**, which means optimizing its internal parameters (weights) to minimize errors and improve its ability to generate content.
   - The **training process** involves feeding data into the model and adjusting its weights using **optimization algorithms**. The most common algorithm used in generative AI is **Stochastic Gradient Descent (SGD)**, along with variations like **Adam** (Adaptive Moment

Estimation), which help adjust the learning rate and improve convergence.

- o During training, the model's performance is evaluated using a **loss function** that quantifies how well the model is generating content. The optimizer uses the loss to update the model's parameters in a way that reduces the error and improves the quality of the generated outputs.
- o Training can take a long time, especially for large models, and may require a lot of computational power (e.g., GPUs or TPUs) to process large datasets efficiently.

Understanding the Training Process of GPT, GANs, and Diffusion Models

Different types of generative AI models require different training strategies and architectures. Let's dive into how **GPT, GANs,** and **Diffusion models** are trained:

1. **Training GPT (Generative Pretrained Transformer)**:
   - o **GPT** models are based on the **transformer architecture**, which is particularly well-suited for handling sequences of data, like text. Training a GPT model involves two primary steps:

- **Pretraining**: The model is trained on a large corpus of text (such as books, articles, and websites) to predict the next word in a sequence of text. This pretraining step allows GPT to learn patterns in language, including grammar, syntax, and even facts about the world.
- **Fine-tuning**: After pretraining, GPT models are fine-tuned for specific tasks, such as **question answering**, **text summarization**, or **dialog generation**. Fine-tuning involves training the model on a smaller, task-specific dataset to optimize its performance for that task.

○ The training process for GPT models requires **large-scale computing resources** due to the size of the model and the amount of data it is trained on.

2. **Training GANs (Generative Adversarial Networks)**:
   ○ GANs are based on an adversarial framework where two neural networks—the **generator** and the **discriminator**—are trained simultaneously.
   - **Generator**: The generator creates fake content (such as images, text, or audio) from random noise.
   - **Discriminator**: The discriminator evaluates the content,

distinguishing between real and fake data.

o During training, the **generator** learns to create more convincing content by trying to **fool the discriminator**, while the **discriminator** becomes better at detecting fake content.

o The model is trained using a process called **backpropagation**, where the generator and discriminator adjust their weights based on the loss function. The generator tries to minimize the loss by creating more realistic content, and the discriminator minimizes its loss by improving its ability to classify content.

o **Challenges**: Training GANs can be difficult due to issues like **mode collapse** (where the generator produces a limited variety of outputs) and the balance between the generator and discriminator. Fine-tuning these models requires careful monitoring to ensure both networks improve in sync.

3. **Training Diffusion Models**:

o Diffusion models work by progressively adding **noise** to data and then training the model to reverse this process, generating high-quality images or other data from random noise.

o The process can be broken down into two stages:

▪ **Forward Process**: During training, noise is gradually added to an image (or other data) in a series of steps, transforming it into random noise. The model learns how this noise is added at each step.

- **Reverse Process**: The model is then trained to reverse this process by **denoising** the data, progressively recovering the original content from the noisy data. The model learns to generate high-quality images by denoising in multiple steps.

o Diffusion models require large datasets and extensive computational resources due to the complexity of the reverse process and the number of training steps involved.

o These models are particularly effective for generating high-quality, detailed images from random noise, making them a popular choice for text-to-image generation.

Real-World Example: Training a Basic Text-to-Image Generator

Let's look at a practical example: training a basic **text-to-image generator** using **Generative AI**. We'll outline the steps involved in training a model like **Stable Diffusion** or a simple version of **GAN** for image generation.

1. **Step 1: Data Preparation**:
   - **Dataset**: Gather a large dataset of images along with descriptive text captions. Datasets like **COCO (Common Objects in Context)** or **LAION** can be used, which contain thousands of labeled images and their corresponding captions.
   - **Preprocessing**: Preprocess the images by resizing them to a consistent size, normalizing pixel values, and converting the text captions into a format that the model can understand (e.g., tokenizing text).
2. **Step 2: Choosing the Architecture**:
   - For a simple text-to-image model, we might choose to use a **GAN** or a **Variational Autoencoder (VAE)** with a conditioning mechanism that incorporates the text as input.
   - **Conditioning on Text**: To make the model generate images based on text descriptions, we need to **condition** the model on the text input. This could be done by feeding the tokenized text into an **embedding layer** and using that to guide the generation process.
3. **Step 3: Training the Model**:
   - The model is trained by feeding pairs of images and captions into the network. The generator learns to produce images that match the textual description, and the discriminator or other evaluative mechanism helps refine the output.

- o Use an **optimization algorithm** like Adam to update the model's weights, minimizing the loss function (which measures how far the generated image is from the true image).
4. **Step 4: Evaluation and Fine-Tuning**:
    - o Once the model has been trained, it is evaluated on its ability to generate images based on new text descriptions. Fine-tuning might be necessary to improve the quality and diversity of generated images.
    - o Techniques like **inception score** or **Fréchet Inception Distance (FID)** are often used to measure the quality of generated images.

Summary

In this chapter, we covered the fundamental steps involved in **training generative AI models**. We explored the importance of **data preparation**, the design of the **model architecture**, and the role of **optimization** in ensuring that generative models produce high-quality content. Additionally, we discussed how models like **GPT**, **GANs**, and **Diffusion models** are trained to generate text, images, and other forms of content, each with its own unique approach.

Through the example of training a **basic text-to-image generator**, we saw how generative models can learn to create realistic content by analyzing vast amounts of data, refining their understanding of patterns, and iterating on their outputs until they can generate high-quality, diverse results.

CHAPTER TWENTY

Model Deployment and Scaling

How to Deploy AI Models for Production Use

Deploying AI models for production use involves transitioning a model from a research or development environment to an operational system where it can serve real users in real-time. This process is critical for ensuring that AI models are scalable, efficient, and reliable when used in real-world applications. In this section, we will explore the steps involved in deploying generative AI models for production use.

1. **Model Export and Packaging**:
   o Once the AI model is trained and performs well on validation data, it needs to be **exported** and **packaged** for deployment. This usually involves saving the trained model in a specific format (e.g., **ONNX, TensorFlow SavedModel, PyTorch model checkpoint**) that can be loaded and used in production systems.
   o The model needs to be **optimized** for inference, which is the process of running predictions or generating outputs. **Quantization** (reducing the precision of the model's weights) and **pruning** (removing redundant or less important parameters) are techniques that help

reduce the model size and speed up inference.

2. **Setting Up Inference Infrastructure**:
   o **Inference servers** are set up to handle requests from end-users or applications. This could be done using cloud-based services like **AWS Sagemaker**, **Google AI Platform**, or **Microsoft Azure Machine Learning** for easier scaling and management. Alternatively, you can use dedicated **on-premises infrastructure** for more control over the deployment environment.
   o The inference infrastructure must be able to handle the computational demands of the AI model, which may require specialized hardware such as **GPUs** or **TPUs** for faster processing, especially for generative models that can be resource-intensive.

3. **API Endpoints**:
   o The deployed model is typically exposed via **API endpoints**. These endpoints accept input data, pass it to the model for processing, and return the results to the user. For example, a **RESTful API** or **gRPC** can be used to expose the model, allowing users or applications to send requests and receive responses.
   o API security is crucial when deploying AI models to ensure that the system is protected against unauthorized access or misuse. Implementing authentication and

authorization protocols (e.g., **OAuth** or **API keys**) is important to secure the deployed model.

4. **Scaling for High Traffic**:
   o As the number of requests to the AI model increases, you may need to **scale** the infrastructure to handle the load. This can be done by adding more **instances** of the model or distributing the load across multiple **servers** or **containers**.
   o **Auto-scaling** tools like **Kubernetes** or **AWS Elastic Beanstalk** can be used to automatically adjust the number of instances based on incoming traffic, ensuring that the model can handle varying loads efficiently.

Deployment Challenges with Generative Models

While deploying generative AI models can provide significant benefits, it also comes with several unique challenges. These challenges stem from the complex nature of generative models and their resource-intensive requirements.

1. **Latency and Real-Time Performance**:
   o Generative models, particularly those based on **deep learning**, can require significant computational resources, making them slow for real-time inference. Generating high-quality content, such as

text or images, can involve complex operations, leading to latency issues.

- o To mitigate this, techniques like **model quantization, distillation** (training smaller, more efficient models), and **batching** (processing multiple requests together) are often used to speed up inference. Additionally, deploying the model on **specialized hardware** (like GPUs or TPUs) can significantly reduce inference time.

2. **Model Size and Resource Consumption**:
   - o Generative models, especially large models like **GPT-3** or **Stable Diffusion**, are typically very large, requiring significant storage space and memory for deployment. This can make it challenging to deploy the model on devices with limited resources, such as smartphones or edge devices.
   - o **Model compression techniques** and **distributed inference** (splitting the model across multiple devices) are often used to mitigate these challenges. In cloud environments, models can be deployed with more flexibility, but there is still a need to ensure efficient use of resources to avoid excessive costs.

3. **Data Privacy and Compliance**:
   - o Deploying generative AI models often involves handling sensitive user data. For example, models that generate text may need to process user queries or data, and

models used in healthcare may handle medical information.

- o Ensuring **data privacy** and compliance with regulations like **GDPR** (General Data Protection Regulation) and **HIPAA** (Health Insurance Portability and Accountability Act) is essential. AI models should be designed with **data anonymization** techniques, and appropriate security measures should be in place to protect data during transmission and storage.

4. **Continuous Monitoring and Maintenance**:

- o Once deployed, AI models require **continuous monitoring** to ensure that they are performing well and providing accurate results. This is especially important for generative models, as they might produce outputs that are unexpected or biased.
- o **Model drift** is another concern, where the model's performance can degrade over time as the underlying data distribution changes. Regular **retraining** or **fine-tuning** may be required to keep the model up-to-date and accurate.

Real-World Example: Serving GPT for Scalable Customer Support

A real-world example of deploying a **generative AI model** for scalable production use is **GPT-powered**

customer support systems. Companies are increasingly using large language models like **GPT-3** to automate customer support tasks, such as answering queries, providing information, and even resolving issues through conversational agents or chatbots.

1. **Deployment in Customer Support**:
   - **Customer support systems** can leverage GPT to provide **instant responses** to customer queries, reducing wait times and increasing the efficiency of the support team. When deployed in production, the GPT model is integrated into the company's **chatbots**, which interact with customers in real-time.
   - For example, a **telecommunications company** might use GPT to respond to frequently asked questions about billing, account management, and technical troubleshooting. By deploying the model via **API endpoints**, the chatbot can send customer queries to the model, receive responses, and deliver them to the user instantly.

2. **Handling Scaling and Traffic**:
   - A large company with thousands of customers might experience high traffic to its customer support system, especially during peak hours. To manage this, the infrastructure needs to be **scalable**, ensuring that the model can handle a high volume of simultaneous requests without crashing or slowing down.

- o **Auto-scaling** solutions, such as **Kubernetes** or **AWS Lambda**, are used to automatically adjust the number of model instances based on demand, ensuring that the system remains responsive even during traffic spikes.

3. **Challenges and Solutions**:
   - o **Latency**: To ensure real-time responses, GPT models may be optimized through **model compression** or **distillation** techniques. These techniques reduce the size of the model while maintaining accuracy, making it faster to serve customer queries.
   - o **Content Moderation**: Since generative models can produce unexpected or inappropriate content, companies often implement moderation systems to filter out harmful responses. AI models may be combined with **content moderation filters** that prevent inappropriate language, ensuring that responses align with company policies.

4. **Continuous Monitoring and Improvement**:
   - o After deployment, the performance of the AI model is continuously monitored to ensure the quality of responses. **User feedback** is collected to identify areas where the model might be underperforming, and periodic **retraining** is done to fine-tune the model with new data or address emerging customer concerns.

    o   Additionally, **A/B testing** can be used to experiment with different versions of the model and refine it over time based on performance metrics.

Summary

In this chapter, we explored the complexities involved in **deploying generative AI models** for production use, focusing on steps such as **model packaging**, **infrastructure setup**, and **scaling** for real-time applications. We discussed the challenges specific to generative models, including **latency**, **resource consumption**, and **data privacy**, as well as strategies to overcome them, such as **model quantization, batch processing**, and **data anonymization**.

Through the example of deploying **GPT for customer support**, we saw how AI can be scaled to handle high traffic, automate responses, and continuously improve based on user interactions. The deployment of AI in customer support is just one of many applications where generative models are making a significant impact, offering businesses the ability to automate and scale their operations efficiently.

CHAPTER TWENTYONE

Combining Generative AI Models: Multimodal Systems

What Are Multimodal AI Systems?

Multimodal AI systems are artificial intelligence models that can process and generate multiple types of data, such as **text**, **images**, **audio**, and **video**, simultaneously. These systems are designed to integrate diverse inputs and outputs into a single cohesive model, allowing for more complex, human-like interactions. Unlike traditional AI models that focus on one modality (e.g., natural language processing or image recognition), multimodal models combine several modalities to better understand context, create richer outputs, and offer more advanced capabilities.

1. **Why Multimodal AI?**
   - o Humans experience the world through multiple senses—sight, sound, touch, etc. To make AI more powerful and human-like, multimodal systems attempt to replicate this sensory integration by using different data types (such as text, images, and audio) together to provide more comprehensive insights and responses.
   - o Multimodal AI allows models to handle complex tasks that require understanding of multiple forms of data at once. For

example, generating a video from a text prompt involves processing both text (for context) and visual/audio data (for the final output). These models are also better at mimicking human communication, where we often combine language, visuals, and sound to convey meaning.

2. **Types of Modalities in AI**:
   - **Text**: Natural language text, including speech-to-text and text-to-speech technologies, is one of the most common modalities in AI, used for tasks like language translation, content generation, and customer service.
   - **Images**: Image recognition, generation, and processing enable AI to understand and create visual content. This modality is widely used in computer vision tasks such as facial recognition, object detection, and image captioning.
   - **Audio**: Speech recognition and generation are crucial for systems that interact with users through voice commands or responses. This modality is used in virtual assistants and music generation.
   - **Video**: Video combines both visual and audio data, making it one of the most complex modalities to process. Video AI applications include surveillance, video generation, and media analysis.

How to Combine Text, Image, Audio, and Video in One System

Combining multiple modalities into a unified system involves integrating different types of data processing models into a cohesive framework. The key challenge is ensuring that each modality's information is appropriately processed and synthesized, allowing the system to produce accurate and coherent outputs. Here's how this can be done:

1. **Unified Models for Multimodal Integration**:
   - One approach to combining modalities is to use a **shared embedding space**, where different modalities (text, images, audio) are mapped into a common representation. This enables the model to process all modalities together, capturing relationships across them. For example, in a multimodal chatbot, the model might generate a text response while also selecting relevant images or audio clips based on the conversation.
   - **Multimodal transformers** (like **CLIP** for images and text or **VisualBERT** for image and text tasks) are becoming more common in multimodal AI. These models are trained on datasets that contain paired data (e.g., images with descriptive text) to help the model learn the relationships between modalities.
2. **Text-to-Image/Video Generation**:

o Combining **text** and **images** or **video** is an exciting area of generative AI. For example, **text-to-image models** (like **DALL·E** or **Stable Diffusion**) can generate realistic images based on text prompts, while **text-to-video models** (like **Make-A-Video**) extend this by generating animated videos from textual descriptions.

o In text-to-video systems, the model not only needs to understand the **text** but also generate sequences of frames that match the description over time, ensuring smooth transitions, contextual accuracy, and consistency in the video's narrative.

3. **Audio and Visual Integration**:

o Combining **audio** and **visual data** is especially useful in applications like **speech-driven video generation** or **lip-syncing technology**. AI models can learn to generate videos where the characters' mouth movements sync up with the speech, producing realistic animations.

o **Multimodal AI systems** can also be used in virtual environments or gaming to synchronize characters' movements, expressions, and voiceovers, making the interaction more engaging and realistic. For instance, a video game character's speech and actions can be driven by the combination of textual input (dialogue), audio output (speech), and visual output (animations).

4. **Training Multimodal Models**:
   - Training multimodal models involves large-scale datasets that contain multiple modalities. For example, a **multimodal AI model** might be trained on a dataset of **videos** that have both **audio** and **text captions**, enabling the model to learn how to align spoken words, text, and visuals.
   - **Contrastive learning** is often used to train these models, where the system learns to associate corresponding modalities, such as matching a text description with the correct image or video frame. This is especially important for tasks like image captioning, where the model needs to correlate visual elements with descriptive language.

5. **Generative AI in Video and Audio Production**:
   - **Generative AI** is increasingly being used in the **media and entertainment industries** to create realistic **audio-visual content**. AI can generate new **soundtracks** or **video sequences** based on a user's text input. This is especially useful for content creators looking to produce videos, advertisements, or social media content at scale without the need for large teams or expensive equipment.
   - The system might take a written script, generate a video based on the script, and then generate voiceovers or background music that match the tone of the video.

This seamless integration of multiple modalities is what makes these systems incredibly powerful for creative professionals.

Real-World Example: AI-Powered Virtual Assistants like Siri and Alexa

Virtual assistants such as **Siri**, **Alexa**, and **Google Assistant** are prime examples of multimodal AI systems that combine **text**, **audio**, and **video** (to some extent) to provide rich, personalized user experiences.

1. **Text and Speech Interaction**:
    - Virtual assistants rely heavily on **speech recognition** and **natural language processing (NLP)** to understand user commands and generate appropriate responses. The **audio** modality (user speech) is converted into **text**, which is then processed by the assistant's **AI model** to understand the intent behind the command.
    - Once the system understands the user's request, it generates a **text-based response**, which is then converted back into **speech** for the user. This interaction requires highly efficient speech-to-text and text-to-speech systems, often powered by AI-driven models.
2. **Audio-Visual Interaction (Smart Displays)**:

- o Virtual assistants like **Amazon Echo Show** or **Google Nest Hub** feature **smart displays** that combine **audio** and **visual** outputs. In these systems, the assistant can respond to a voice query not only with speech but also by displaying relevant information on the screen. For example, a user might ask about the weather, and the assistant will reply verbally while showing a weather forecast graphic.
- o In more advanced versions, AI can be used to provide **real-time video responses**. For example, asking the assistant to play a specific video or tutorial on YouTube or a cooking demonstration.

3. **Contextual Awareness and Multimodal Integration**:
   - o Virtual assistants are increasingly capable of understanding **contextual** information from multiple data streams. For instance, when asking Alexa to "turn off the lights," the assistant might combine the audio input with data from connected devices (like smart home lights) to execute the command.
   - o Some assistants also use **camera feeds** (via smart cameras or phones) to enhance their understanding of user commands. This can include **face recognition** or detecting what is happening in the environment to respond more appropriately. For example, a virtual

assistant might identify the user's face and tailor its responses based on who is asking the question.

4. **Training Multimodal Assistants**:
   - These systems rely on large-scale multimodal datasets that combine **text**, **speech**, and sometimes **visual data** (like images, gestures, or video frames). By using these datasets, virtual assistants can be trained to improve the accuracy of their responses, better recognize accents, and handle diverse speech patterns or commands.

Summary

In this chapter, we explored the fascinating world of **multimodal AI systems** that integrate different types of data—text, images, audio, and video—into cohesive, intelligent models. These systems are becoming more prevalent in applications like **virtual assistants**, where multiple modalities (text, voice, and visual output) work together to provide seamless, personalized user experiences.

We discussed how combining these modalities can enhance generative AI, allowing for more dynamic, context-aware responses, whether generating images from text or creating immersive, interactive media. The integration of **text**, **audio**, and **visuals** is revolutionizing industries like entertainment, customer service, and smart home technology.

As multimodal AI continues to evolve, it will enable even more advanced, responsive, and creative applications, blurring the lines between human-like interaction and machine intelligence.

CHAPTER TWENTYTWO

Challenges and Future of Generative AI

Current Challenges in Generative AI: Quality, Ethical Concerns, and Data Issues

As **Generative AI** continues to grow in popularity and capability, it faces several challenges that need to be addressed to ensure the technology's responsible and effective use. These challenges range from **quality control** to **ethical concerns** and **data-related issues**. Let's break down some of the primary obstacles currently faced by generative AI models.

1. **Quality of Generated Content**:
   o **Inconsistency**: Generative AI models, especially when trained on massive datasets, can sometimes produce content that is inconsistent or lacks coherence. For example, in text generation, AI might produce fluent text in some cases, but in others, it might produce nonsensical or off-topic sentences.
   o **Creativity vs. Originality**: While AI models like **GPT-3** can generate creative and seemingly original content, they can also struggle with genuinely novel ideas. Since these models are trained on existing data, their outputs may often resemble combinations of what they have already

seen rather than introducing truly innovative content.

- o **Hallucination**: Generative models can sometimes "hallucinate" information, meaning they produce facts or details that are not true, such as making up non-existent statistics, people, or events. This is particularly problematic in fields like healthcare or legal advice, where accuracy is critical.

2. **Ethical Concerns**:

- o **Bias in AI**: Generative AI models learn from the data they are trained on, which can include **biased**, **discriminatory**, or **harmful** content. For example, a text-generation model might generate content that perpetuates racial, gender, or cultural biases present in its training data. Addressing bias is one of the most pressing ethical challenges in AI development.

- o **Deepfakes and Misinformation**: One of the most well-known ethical concerns with generative AI is its ability to produce **deepfakes**—realistic but fake audio, video, or images that can deceive viewers. This poses risks to **trust** in media, especially when it comes to **news** and **political content**, where misleading information can be generated to manipulate public opinion.

- o **Copyright and Ownership**: The rise of AI-generated content also raises questions about **authorship** and **intellectual property**. Who owns content generated by an AI? The person who provided the prompt, the developers of the AI model, or the AI itself? These questions complicate how AI-generated art, literature, and music are treated under current copyright laws.

3. **Data Issues**:
   - **Data Privacy**: Many generative AI models, particularly those used in healthcare, finance, or customer service, process sensitive data. Ensuring that these models comply with **data privacy regulations** like **GDPR** and **HIPAA** is a major concern. AI models must be designed to protect personal data and avoid mishandling sensitive information.
   - **Quality and Diversity of Training Data**: The quality of a generative AI model is directly tied to the quality and diversity of the data it is trained on. If the training data is narrow or unrepresentative, the AI's output will be similarly limited. For instance, an AI trained mostly on Western media might struggle to generate content that reflects other cultures or perspectives. Moreover, poor-quality or inaccurate data can lead to poor model performance or "garbage in, garbage out" outcomes.

Emerging Research in the Field of Generative Models

The field of generative AI is rapidly evolving, with ongoing research aimed at improving the quality, safety, and efficiency of AI models. Some of the most exciting directions in generative AI research include:

1. **Improving Model Accuracy and Consistency**:
   o Researchers are focusing on ways to reduce **model hallucination** and improve the accuracy of the outputs generated by AI. This includes techniques like **fine-tuning**, where models are specifically trained on curated datasets to increase their relevance and reliability for specific tasks.
   o **Reinforcement learning from human feedback (RLHF)** is an emerging area where AI models are trained to align better with human preferences by learning from direct human input. This method helps improve model outputs, making them more natural and useful.
2. **Generative Models for Multimodal Content**:
   o As discussed in earlier chapters, the combination of text, image, video, and audio generation in **multimodal AI systems** is a growing area of research. Models that can seamlessly integrate and generate outputs across different modalities are being developed to handle more complex tasks, such as generating realistic video and audio from a single

text prompt or creating interactive environments based on both visual and audio inputs.

- o The research focuses on improving the **alignment** between these modalities to ensure that the content generated is coherent across text, images, and sounds, offering a more realistic and engaging experience.

3. **Ethical AI and Bias Mitigation**:
   - o Addressing ethical concerns, such as **bias reduction** and **fairness**, is a key area of current research. New techniques are being developed to better identify and mitigate biases in the training data and model outputs. **Fairness-aware learning algorithms** are being designed to ensure that generative models do not perpetuate harmful stereotypes or make biased decisions based on race, gender, or other factors.
   - o Additionally, researchers are working on methods for **explainability** in AI, which aims to make AI systems more transparent and understandable, so users and developers can better understand how decisions are made and identify potential ethical issues.

4. **Energy-Efficiency and Sustainability**:
   - o Generative AI models, particularly large models like GPT-3 and DALL·E, are **resource-intensive** and require significant computational power for both

training and inference. Researchers are exploring ways to make these models more **energy-efficient** and reduce their **carbon footprint**.

o Techniques like **model pruning**, **distillation**, and **quantization** help reduce the size of the models and improve their inference speed, thus making them more sustainable and accessible for widespread use.

Real-World Example: Challenges in Scaling AI Models for Mass Use

Scaling generative AI models for mass use comes with several technical, logistical, and ethical challenges. One of the most prominent real-world examples of these challenges is the deployment and scaling of **GPT-3** or similar large-scale generative models.

1. **Technical Challenges in Scaling**:
   o **Infrastructure**: Models like GPT-3 are massive, with billions of parameters. Serving these models requires specialized hardware, such as **GPUs** or **TPUs**, and sophisticated cloud infrastructure to ensure low-latency responses and high availability.
   o **Resource Consumption**: The computational resources needed to train and serve these models are expensive. For example, it can cost millions of dollars to

train a model like GPT-3, and serving the model at scale requires ongoing investment in cloud computing power.

- o **Latency**: Generative models often suffer from **latency issues**, especially when the models are large. Reducing the time it takes to generate content while maintaining the quality of the output is a constant challenge. Optimizing these models for faster response times without sacrificing quality is an ongoing area of research.

2. **Ethical and Governance Concerns in Mass Deployment**:

- o As generative AI models become more powerful and widely used, they also raise concerns about **misuse**. For example, the ability to generate text that mimics human speech can be used for **malicious purposes** such as **phishing**, **fake news generation**, or creating **deepfakes**.

- o **Content Moderation**: Ensuring that generative AI models do not produce harmful, biased, or inappropriate content is crucial, especially when deployed at scale. **Content moderation systems** need to be in place to flag and prevent harmful outputs, but these systems need to be constantly updated to handle the diverse and evolving nature of AI-generated content.

3. **Access and Equity**:

- o **Access to generative AI models** is another challenge. Large companies or well-funded startups may have the resources to train and deploy these models, while smaller organizations or developing nations may lack the infrastructure to harness the power of AI. Ensuring **equitable access** to these technologies is an ongoing concern for the AI community.
- o Additionally, the cost of using these models for businesses (via APIs, for example) can be prohibitive for some companies, which limits their potential to reach a broader audience.

Summary

In this chapter, we discussed the **current challenges** facing generative AI, including issues related to **quality**, **ethics**, and **data privacy**. We also examined **emerging research** that is addressing these challenges, including efforts to improve the accuracy of AI outputs, reduce bias, and enhance sustainability. Finally, we looked at a **real-world example** of the challenges involved in **scaling AI models** for mass use, particularly focusing on the complexities of deploying large models like **GPT-3** in real-world applications.

As generative AI continues to evolve, it will be critical to address these challenges to ensure that these models are used responsibly, efficiently, and for the benefit of all. The future of generative AI holds immense potential, but it will require careful research, governance, and thoughtful development to navigate these hurdles effectively.

CHAPTER TWENTYTHREE

Creative Applications of Generative AI: Art, Fashion, and Design

How Generative AI is Shaping the Future of Creative Industries

Generative AI has made a significant impact on the creative industries, transforming how art, fashion, architecture, and design are produced. By leveraging the power of machine learning models that can generate new content based on input data, creatives can now explore new possibilities, streamline their workflows, and experiment with innovative designs in ways that were previously unimaginable.

1. **Creativity Augmented by AI**:
   o Traditionally, creativity in fields like art, fashion, and design was solely in the hands of human artists and designers. However, generative AI allows these creators to collaborate with machines to push the boundaries of what is possible. These models don't replace human creativity but act as **tools** that enhance and accelerate the creative process, offering new perspectives and ideas.
   o AI-generated content can take many forms, including **visual art, fashion designs, architectural blueprints,**

advertisements, and even **music**. By training on vast datasets of existing works, AI models can produce novel pieces that combine elements from various sources, resulting in innovative and diverse outputs.

2. **AI as a Collaborative Tool**:
   - In the creative process, AI can serve as a **co-creator**, generating initial drafts or ideas that artists and designers can refine and build upon. For example, a painter might use a generative model to create a base image that they can then modify and personalize, while a fashion designer might use AI to create a fabric pattern that serves as the foundation for a new collection.
   - AI models also enable **rapid iteration** in design processes. In fashion, architecture, and art, AI tools can generate hundreds of potential designs in seconds, allowing creatives to test multiple ideas quickly before deciding on the best direction.

3. **Customization and Personalization**:
   - Generative AI is enabling a level of **personalization** that was previously difficult to achieve at scale. In industries like fashion and design, AI can create custom products tailored to individual tastes, body types, or preferences. For example, AI-powered tools can generate fashion items or accessories based on a user's specific measurements, style

preferences, and previous purchases, providing a more personalized shopping experience.

o In art, AI can help create **customized pieces** based on a client's preferences or even create unique **artworks on demand**, reflecting personal themes, color palettes, and emotional tones.

AI in Fashion Design, Architecture, and Advertising

Generative AI is increasingly being used in **fashion**, **architecture**, and **advertising**, helping to streamline design processes, enhance creativity, and introduce novel approaches to problem-solving.

1. **AI in Fashion Design**:
   o AI models in fashion design can generate patterns, color schemes, and entire garment designs. By training on extensive fashion databases, these AI tools can learn to produce new, innovative fashion items that are in line with current trends or completely original concepts.
   o **Generative design tools** in fashion also help reduce waste by optimizing patterns for fabric cutting, ensuring that materials are used efficiently. AI can suggest design alterations that minimize the environmental impact while maximizing style and functionality.

- o **AI in textile design** can create unique fabrics with customized textures, patterns, and even sustainability features. AI tools can simulate how different fabrics will behave and generate virtual prototypes for designers to assess before producing physical samples.

2. **AI in Architecture**:
   - o In **architecture**, generative AI is used to explore new forms, structures, and spatial layouts. By using **generative design** techniques, AI can propose hundreds of design options based on certain constraints (e.g., size, location, materials). Architects can use AI to generate optimized building designs that maximize space utilization, energy efficiency, and environmental sustainability.
   - o AI can also assist in **structural analysis**, predicting how a building will respond to environmental factors like wind, rain, or seismic activity, allowing architects to create safer and more resilient designs.
   - o **Generative architecture** is revolutionizing urban planning, enabling the creation of complex cities and public spaces that are optimized for both functionality and aesthetic appeal.

3. **AI in Advertising**:
   - o In **advertising**, generative AI is transforming how campaigns are created and personalized. AI can generate

multiple variations of ads (from text-based copy to visual and video content) tailored to specific demographics, resulting in more targeted and engaging advertisements.

- o **AI-driven content generation tools** can create unique social media posts, email marketing campaigns, and digital banners based on user data and behavior. This helps brands reach their audiences more effectively by delivering personalized content that aligns with the interests and needs of individual customers.
- o **AI-powered video and audio editing tools** can streamline the process of creating promotional videos and jingles, producing high-quality content that can be customized on the fly.

Real-World Example: AI-Generated Fashion and Digital Art Exhibitions

Generative AI has already begun to make waves in the world of **fashion design** and **digital art**, with several real-world examples highlighting the potential and impact of these technologies.

1. **AI-Generated Fashion**:
   - o In 2021, **Balenciaga** and **H&M** were among the fashion brands experimenting with AI in their design processes. Balenciaga collaborated with an AI

company to create virtual clothing collections, exploring new ways to blend **AI-generated designs** with traditional craftsmanship.

o **The Fabricant**, a digital fashion house, specializes in creating entirely **AI-generated fashion** that exists only in the digital world. They create **virtual fashion pieces** and host **digital-only fashion shows**, catering to the growing market of **virtual influencers** and users of **virtual reality (VR)** and **augmented reality (AR)** platforms. AI is used to generate unique textures, patterns, and 3D models of garments, and these creations can be worn by avatars in virtual environments.

o AI is also being used to generate **customized fashion items**. For example, brands like **Stitch Fix** use AI to analyze customer data (such as preferences, body type, and past purchases) to generate personalized clothing recommendations and even design items tailored to each customer's needs.

2. **AI-Generated Digital Art Exhibitions**:

o AI-generated art is gaining recognition in galleries and exhibitions around the world. In 2018, an AI-generated artwork titled **"Portrait of Edmond de Belamy"** was sold at **Christie's Auction House** for over \$432,000. The portrait was created by **Obvious**, a French collective, using a

GAN model trained on historical portraits.

- o **AI Art Exhibitions** have become more common, with AI-generated art being showcased in both traditional galleries and online platforms. Artists and technologists are exploring how generative AI can help create entirely new forms of art by combining style and technique in novel ways. The **AI art movement** continues to grow, with artists using AI tools to create everything from abstract paintings to hyper-realistic portraits.

- o **Generative AI models** can create images based on text prompts, leading to interactive art exhibitions where visitors can input their own descriptions and see the AI generate corresponding visual works. These exhibitions raise questions about the nature of authorship, originality, and creativity in the age of AI.

3. **AI in Video Games and Virtual Worlds**:
   - o In addition to fashion and visual art, AI is also being used to create virtual environments and characters in video games. Generative AI can design **unique, procedurally generated** worlds that evolve in real-time based on player interactions.

   - o For example, in **No Man's Sky**, AI generates entire planets, ecosystems, and biomes, providing an ever-expanding universe for players to explore. AI-generated content is not just confined to static art—it's dynamically created, offering infinite possibilities for game designers and players alike.

Summary

In this chapter, we explored the **creative applications of generative AI** in industries like **art, fashion, architecture**, and **advertising**. Generative AI is reshaping these fields by enabling faster, more personalized design processes, encouraging collaboration between humans and machines, and creating entirely new forms of creative expression.

We discussed how AI is being used to generate **fashion designs, virtual environments**, and **art**, as well as how these technologies are already being showcased in **digital art exhibitions** and **fashion shows**. With the help of AI, designers and artists can explore limitless creative possibilities, while industries can scale their operations to create customized, efficient, and sustainable products.

The future of **generative AI in creativity** holds exciting opportunities, from **AI-driven fashion collections** to **immersive virtual art worlds**, paving the way for new forms of self-expression and pushing the boundaries of what is possible in the creative industries.

CHAPTER TWENTYFOUR

Building Your Own AI Models with Open-Source Tools

A Guide to Open-Source Frameworks: TensorFlow, PyTorch, HuggingFace

Open-source tools have become the cornerstone of AI and machine learning development. These frameworks provide a wide range of features, libraries, and resources that allow anyone—from beginners to experts—to build, train, and deploy AI models. In this section, we'll introduce three of the most popular open-source frameworks for building generative models: **TensorFlow**, **PyTorch**, and **HuggingFace**.

1. **TensorFlow**:
   - **Overview**: **TensorFlow**, developed by **Google**, is one of the most widely-used open-source frameworks for machine learning. It offers robust support for building and deploying **deep learning** models, particularly those requiring large-scale computations.
   - **Strengths**:
     - Highly scalable and optimized for distributed computing.
     - Excellent support for both training and production deployment (especially on Google Cloud).

- Built-in tools for deploying models to mobile, web, and embedded devices.
  o **Use in Generative Models**: TensorFlow is widely used for training **GANs, VAEs**, and other generative models. The framework includes high-level libraries like **TensorFlow Keras**, which makes it easier to define and train complex models.
  o **Example**: TensorFlow can be used to create models like **StyleGAN** for generating high-quality images, or **Transformer-based models** for text generation.

2. **PyTorch**:
   o **Overview**: **PyTorch**, developed by **Facebook**, has gained significant traction in the AI community, particularly for research and prototyping. It is well-known for its **dynamic computation graph**, which makes it more flexible and intuitive to work with.
   o **Strengths**:
     - Easier to debug and experiment with compared to TensorFlow.
     - Better suited for research and development due to its flexibility.
     - Strong community support and excellent documentation.
   o **Use in Generative Models**: PyTorch excels in research-driven models, such as **GANs, VAEs**, and **Transformers**, due to its ease of use and flexibility. Many state-

of-the-art models, including **GPT** and **BERT**, were initially developed using PyTorch.

- o **Example**: PyTorch's **torchgan** library allows for easy creation and training of GANs, while **transformers** can be used to fine-tune large pre-trained models for specific tasks like text generation.

3. **HuggingFace**:

- o **Overview**: **HuggingFace** has become a leader in the natural language processing (NLP) space, providing a library called **Transformers**, which contains a vast number of pre-trained models for tasks like text generation, translation, and summarization.
- o **Strengths**:
  - Large repository of pre-trained models that can be easily downloaded and fine-tuned.
  - Strong support for **Transformer-based models**, such as **GPT-2**, **BERT**, and **T5**.
  - Simple API for training and fine-tuning models on custom datasets.
- o **Use in Generative Models**: HuggingFace excels in training **language models** and offers pre-trained models like **GPT-2**, **GPT-3**, and **BERT** that you can use as starting points for your generative applications.
- o **Example**: HuggingFace makes it easy to fine-tune a **GPT model** on a custom

dataset to generate text for a specific domain, such as generating customer support dialogues or creating product descriptions.

How to Build, Train, and Fine-Tune Your Own Generative Models

Building your own generative AI model involves several key steps: **data collection, model architecture design, training**, and **fine-tuning**. Here's a general guide on how to build, train, and fine-tune your own generative models using open-source tools like TensorFlow, PyTorch, and HuggingFace.

1. **Step 1: Data Collection and Preprocessing**:
   o **Data Collection**: The first step in building any generative model is collecting a relevant and high-quality dataset. For a text-to-image model, you would need a dataset that pairs **text descriptions** with corresponding **images** (e.g., COCO dataset). For a text-generation model, you'd need a large corpus of **text data**.
   o **Preprocessing**: Data must be preprocessed before being used to train the model. This includes tasks like:
     ▪ **Text preprocessing**: Tokenization, lowercasing, removing stop words, etc.

- **Image preprocessing**: Resizing, normalization, and augmentation.
  - o The preprocessing stage is crucial for ensuring that the model receives clean, high-quality input that can be efficiently learned from.

2. **Step 2: Defining the Model Architecture**:
   - o Depending on the type of generative model you're building (e.g., **GAN, VAE, Transformer**), you will need to design the architecture.
     - **GANs** consist of two parts: a **generator** and a **discriminator**. The generator creates content, while the discriminator evaluates it.
     - **VAEs** are designed to learn the latent space of the data and are commonly used for image generation.
     - **Transformer-based models** like **GPT** and **BERT** excel at generating text by learning from large datasets of text and understanding context.
   - o Open-source frameworks like TensorFlow and PyTorch provide pre-built components and layers, making it easier to implement complex architectures.

3. **Step 3: Training the Model**:
   - o **Choosing the right optimizer**: Once the model architecture is defined, the next

step is to train the model. You will need to select an **optimizer** (e.g., **Adam, SGD**) and a **loss function** (e.g., **cross-entropy loss** for text generation or **binary cross-entropy** for GANs).

- o **Training process**: During training, the model will adjust its parameters by using backpropagation to minimize the loss function. The training process can take a long time, especially for large models like **GPT-3**.
- o **Regularization**: To prevent overfitting, regularization techniques such as **dropout** or **L2 regularization** can be applied during training.

4. **Step 4: Fine-Tuning the Model**:
   - o Fine-tuning is the process of adapting a pre-trained model (e.g., a pre-trained **GPT-2** or **GAN**) to a specific task by training it further on a smaller, task-specific dataset.
   - o In **HuggingFace**, fine-tuning is simplified by using pre-trained models and applying transfer learning, where the model is adjusted on a new dataset to specialize in the task.
   - o Fine-tuning allows the model to become more efficient and accurate for a specific application, such as generating domain-specific text or creating custom images.

Real-World Example: Building a Custom GPT Model for Your Project

Let's walk through an example of building a custom **GPT model** for a specific project, such as generating text for a customer support chatbot or creating personalized content for a website.

1. **Step 1: Data Collection**:
   o Gather a dataset of **customer queries** and **support responses**. For example, you could collect previous chat logs, customer service scripts, or publicly available datasets of support conversations.
   o Preprocess the data by tokenizing the text, removing unnecessary punctuation, and standardizing the formatting.
2. **Step 2: Choose a Pre-trained Model**:
   o Use a pre-trained model like **GPT-2** or **GPT-3** from HuggingFace's **Transformers** library. These models are already trained on vast amounts of data and can generate high-quality text.
   o For example, **HuggingFace** provides a simple interface to load **GPT-2**, which can be fine-tuned to generate customer service responses by training it further on your dataset.
3. **Step 3: Fine-Tuning the Model**:
   o Fine-tune the pre-trained GPT model on your customer support dataset. In HuggingFace, you can load your dataset, configure the model for fine-tuning, and

start the training process using the `Trainer` API.

- o During fine-tuning, the model learns to generate responses that are specific to customer service interactions. You can control aspects such as tone, helpfulness, and accuracy based on your dataset.

4. **Step 4: Deploying the Model**:
   - o Once the model is trained and fine-tuned, deploy it as an API using frameworks like **FastAPI** or **Flask**, allowing the chatbot to generate responses in real-time.
   - o Scale the deployment by using cloud services like **AWS** or **Google Cloud** to handle multiple requests simultaneously.

Summary

In this chapter, we explored how to build, train, and fine-tune your own generative AI models using open-source tools such as **TensorFlow**, **PyTorch**, and **HuggingFace**. These frameworks provide a powerful foundation for creating a wide range of generative models, from **GANs** to **transformers**. We also discussed a practical example of building a custom **GPT model** for a project like customer support, demonstrating how you can leverage pre-trained models and fine-tune them for specific tasks.

The ability to build and customize your own generative models opens up endless possibilities for applications in industries such as **customer service, content creation**, and **personalized marketing**. With the right tools and techniques, you can take full advantage of the power of AI to solve real-world problems.

CHAPTER TWENTYFIVE

The Role of AI in Education and Learning

How Generative AI Can Transform Learning Experiences

Generative AI has the potential to revolutionize education by creating more dynamic, personalized, and accessible learning experiences. The ability to generate content and adapt learning materials in real-time based on individual needs opens up exciting possibilities for both students and educators.

1. **Personalized Learning**:
   o Generative AI can analyze a student's progress and learning style to generate personalized content tailored to their specific needs. This includes customizing lessons, quizzes, and practice exercises based on areas where the student may be struggling or excelling.
   o With AI's ability to track a learner's interactions and performance, it can dynamically adjust the difficulty of tasks, introduce new concepts when students are ready, and provide additional resources to reinforce weak areas. This creates an individualized learning journey that adapts as the learner progresses, offering a more **engaging** and **effective** education.

2. **Automating Content Creation**:

- o AI can generate educational content, such as **study guides**, **flashcards**, **practice exams**, and even **customized lesson plans**. For example, an AI can generate practice problems based on a textbook chapter, adapting the questions to the student's skill level.
- o Instructors can use AI tools to automatically create tailored materials that are more aligned with the curriculum. This can save educators significant time while providing high-quality, relevant content that meets each learner's needs.

3. **Interactive and Immersive Learning**:
- o Generative AI can power **interactive learning experiences** that engage students in ways that traditional methods cannot. For instance, AI can be used to create **simulations** or **virtual environments** where students can interact with real-world scenarios, like conducting virtual chemistry experiments or exploring historical events in immersive 3D environments.
- o These **AI-powered simulations** make learning more interactive, allowing students to learn by doing rather than just reading or watching. This type of **experiential learning** can enhance understanding and retention, particularly in complex subjects that benefit from hands-on experience.

4. **AI in Adaptive Learning Platforms**:

- o **Adaptive learning systems** powered by AI allow for real-time adjustments to the educational experience. For example, if a student struggles with a particular concept, the system can recognize this challenge and automatically offer supplementary exercises or explanations to clarify the concept.
- o AI can help assess not just what a student knows but also how they learn, tailoring content and presentation to match cognitive styles. This ensures that students engage with the material in the most effective way for their individual learning preferences, whether they are visual, auditory, or kinesthetic learners.

AI as an Educational Tool: Personalized Tutors, Study Guides, and More

Generative AI is already being used as a powerful **educational tool** across a variety of functions. From **personalized tutoring** to **study guides**, AI is transforming how both students and teachers approach learning. Let's look at how AI is enhancing education.

1. **Personalized Tutors**:
   - o AI-powered **tutors** can provide individualized support for students, offering explanations and guidance on specific topics. These AI tutors work 24/7, offering students the opportunity to

ask questions and receive feedback anytime, without having to wait for a human teacher.

- o For example, **language learning platforms** like **Duolingo** use AI to assess a learner's progress and adjust the difficulty level of lessons accordingly. This ensures that the learner is constantly challenged without feeling overwhelmed, creating a customized experience that suits their pace.

2. **Study Guides and Flashcards**:
   - o Generative AI can create **study guides** based on the content of textbooks, lectures, or online resources. The AI can automatically summarize key points and provide **concise explanations**, making complex concepts easier to digest.
   - o Similarly, AI tools can generate **flashcards** based on the learner's weaknesses. If a student struggles with a particular concept or fact, the AI can create targeted flashcards that focus on reinforcing that knowledge. These flashcards can also be customized to reflect a student's preferred learning style (e.g., including visual aids for visual learners).

3. **Smart Quizzes and Assessments**:
   - o AI can generate **customized quizzes** that assess students' understanding of specific topics. Based on the results of these quizzes, AI can then generate follow-up

exercises or challenges tailored to the student's weaknesses, ensuring continuous progress.

  o Furthermore, AI-powered assessment tools can offer **instant feedback**, highlighting areas where a student is excelling and providing suggestions for areas of improvement. This allows students to address learning gaps in real-time.

4. **Interactive Study Resources**:

  o AI can also generate interactive study resources that engage students in problem-solving and critical thinking. For example, **AI-powered coding platforms** like **Replit** and **Codecademy** provide real-time feedback on code written by students, guiding them through debugging and improving their skills as they learn.

Real-World Example: AI-Generated Educational Content and Interactive Learning

Several real-world examples demonstrate how AI is being used to enhance education by generating customized learning materials and fostering interactive learning environments.

1. **AI-Generated Educational Content in K-12 and Higher Education**:

- o **Socratic by Google** is an example of an AI-powered tool that helps students with homework. By taking a photo of a question, the app uses AI to generate explanations and step-by-step solutions for subjects like math, science, and history.
- o **Knewton**, an adaptive learning platform, uses AI to deliver personalized study plans for students. It dynamically adjusts the difficulty of lessons and recommends study materials based on how well the student is performing, ensuring that the learning pace is always optimized for each individual.

2. **Interactive Learning with AI in STEM Education**:
   - o In **STEM education**, AI is being used to create immersive learning experiences. For instance, **Labster** offers **virtual laboratories** that simulate real-world experiments in science, allowing students to perform lab experiments virtually. These simulations are powered by AI, which adapts the learning experience based on the student's progress and offers hints and guidance when necessary.
   - o Similarly, AI is used in **math tutoring** platforms like **Khan Academy**, which uses adaptive AI algorithms to provide personalized learning paths and content recommendations based on the student's performance. As the student progresses

through exercises, AI adjusts the difficulty of the problems and provides tailored feedback.

3. **AI-Powered Language Learning**:
   o In language learning, AI-powered platforms like **Babbel** and **Rosetta Stone** utilize **speech recognition** and **personalized feedback** to help learners practice speaking and writing in a new language. These platforms use AI to adapt to the learner's proficiency level, providing tailored lessons and practice exercises.
   o Additionally, **AI-powered chatbots** are used in language learning apps to engage students in conversational practice, providing a more natural learning experience.

4. **AI-Powered Virtual Classrooms**:
   o Platforms like **Classcraft** and **DreamBox Learning** leverage AI to gamify learning and create interactive classroom experiences. AI dynamically adapts the learning journey to each student's needs, keeping them engaged while helping them stay on track with their learning objectives.
   o **AI-enabled VR classrooms** offer immersive experiences where students can virtually interact with the learning material. In this setup, AI can create dynamic learning environments where the material adjusts in real-time based on the

student's engagement level and interactions.

Summary

In this chapter, we explored the **role of generative AI** in **education** and how it is transforming the learning experience for both students and teachers. From **personalized tutors** to **custom study guides**, AI is revolutionizing how we approach education, providing dynamic, adaptive, and interactive learning tools.

We discussed how AI is enabling **personalized learning experiences**, automating content creation, and enhancing engagement through **interactive simulations** and **real-time feedback**. Real-world examples like **AI-generated educational content**, **interactive learning platforms**, and **AI-powered language tools** show the vast potential of generative AI in reshaping the future of education.

As AI continues to evolve, the way we learn, teach, and interact with educational content will become increasingly personalized and dynamic, ensuring that every student receives the most effective, tailored learning experience possible.

CHAPTER TWENTYSIX

Collaboration Between Humans and Generative AI

The Importance of Human-AI Collaboration in Creative Work

Generative AI has made significant strides in creative fields, but the most powerful and effective applications come from collaboration between **humans** and AI. Rather than replacing creative professionals, AI can act as a **tool** that enhances human creativity, offering new possibilities and methods of expression. The synergy between human intuition, imagination, and AI's computational power leads to groundbreaking works in fields such as **art, music, writing**, and **design**.

1. **AI as a Co-Creator**:
   - The traditional view of creativity often involved human artists working alone, generating ideas, and executing them by hand. However, with AI's ability to **generate new content, analyze large datasets**, and **automate repetitive tasks**, it can now serve as a **co-creator**.
   - In this collaborative model, AI is seen as a partner that **stimulates new ideas**, **suggests variations**, or **produces drafts** that humans can refine. This collaborative approach opens up new avenues for creative professionals, allowing them to

focus more on **concept development** and **refinement** while AI handles time-consuming aspects of content creation.

2. **Human-AI Symbiosis**:
   - AI excels at tasks like **pattern recognition**, **data processing**, and **generating variations**. Humans, on the other hand, bring **intuition**, **emotional intelligence**, and the ability to make **complex aesthetic decisions**. By combining the strengths of both, creative work becomes more efficient and diverse.
   - For example, AI can analyze an artist's previous works and generate new compositions in their style, helping the artist explore variations of their own aesthetic. The artist can then choose the best option, refine it, and make final adjustments, producing a piece that would have taken much longer without AI's assistance.

3. **Breaking Down Creative Barriers**:
   - AI enables individuals to **access creative tools** that might have been previously out of reach. For instance, someone with no formal training in art or music can use AI to generate high-quality creations, lowering the barrier to entry in creative fields.
   - Additionally, AI empowers professionals to **push the boundaries** of their work. Writers can experiment with new styles, musicians can explore unconventional

soundscapes, and visual artists can create interactive experiences that were previously difficult or impossible to achieve.

How AI Can Assist and Augment Human Creativity

Generative AI is not only a tool for creating content but also a powerful assistant that can **augment** the creative process. AI helps by **streamlining workflows**, **suggesting ideas**, and **optimizing content**, allowing humans to focus on higher-level creative tasks. Here's how AI assists human creativity:

1. **Idea Generation and Brainstorming**:
   - AI can be used as a **brainstorming partner**, generating ideas based on input from the creator. For example, writers can use AI to suggest plot twists or character developments based on their initial ideas, while musicians can input a melody and let AI suggest harmonic structures or rhythms.
   - In art, AI models like **DeepArt** or **Artbreeder** can generate visual concepts from a simple text prompt or a rough sketch. These tools help artists explore new directions for their work, creating an expansive pool of ideas to choose from.
2. **Speeding Up Repetitive Tasks**:
   - Creative work often involves repetitive tasks, such as **refining drafts**, **color**

correction, or **mixing sounds**. AI can automate these processes, allowing creatives to spend more time on the **conceptual aspects** of their work.

- For example, in graphic design, AI tools like **Adobe Sensei** can help with automating tasks like image tagging, background removal, or content cropping, freeing up time for the designer to focus on creative decisions.

3. **Enhancing Artistic Expression**:
   - AI is particularly useful in fields that blend **technology** and **art**, such as **interactive art** or **generative music**. In these fields, AI can produce novel outputs that humans can interact with or manipulate, providing a more immersive experience.
   - For instance, in **generative music**, AI can suggest variations in melody, harmony, or instrumentation based on user input, resulting in dynamic and evolving compositions that might not have emerged through traditional methods.
   - Similarly, in **3D design** or **architecture**, AI can assist in creating complex structures, experimenting with different materials, or optimizing designs for environmental sustainability.

4. **Creating Variations and Refinements**:
   - AI can generate multiple **variations** of a design, song, or story, offering creatives the option to select, mix, and refine the

best elements. This is particularly useful in fields like **fashion** and **product design**, where companies can use AI to generate hundreds of design options based on set parameters, such as color, shape, and texture.

o **Musicians** can input basic musical themes and use AI to generate variations in rhythm, instrumentation, or even genres. They can then select the best variations and use them as building blocks for their composition.

Real-World Example: Artists, Writers, and Musicians Using AI as a Tool

Generative AI is already being used in the creative industries, with many artists, writers, and musicians incorporating AI into their workflows. Here are some real-world examples of how AI is augmenting creativity:

1. **Artists Using AI**:
    o **Refik Anadol**, a media artist, uses AI to create stunning **data-driven art**. He applies machine learning algorithms to vast datasets (such as images or videos) to generate immersive, AI-powered visualizations. His works are showcased in prominent museums around the world and represent a fusion of human creativity and machine learning.

- o **Obvious,** a French art collective, created **"Portrait of Edmond de Belamy"**, an AI-generated painting that sold at **Christie's Auction House** for over $432,000. This painting was created using a **GAN**, and the group used the AI as a tool to explore **artificial creativity** and **authorship**.

2. **Writers Using AI:**
   - o **AI in storytelling** has been gaining traction, with writers using tools like **GPT-3** to generate plot ideas, character dialogues, and even complete short stories. For instance, the **AI Dungeon** platform allows users to create their own interactive stories with AI-generated narratives. The AI responds to user inputs, creating unique, evolving stories based on the user's choices.
   - o Writers have also used AI for **co-writing**, where the AI suggests sentences, paragraphs, or even entire chapters. The writer then fine-tunes these suggestions, ensuring the final product aligns with their style and intent. AI can be used to create content across genres, including science fiction, fantasy, and even poetry.

3. **Musicians Using AI:**
   - o **Endlesss,** a music collaboration platform, uses AI to help musicians create real-time collaborative music. The AI listens to the inputs from multiple musicians and generates **loops** and **beats** that fit with the

rhythm and style of the collaboration. This tool allows musicians to experiment with sounds and ideas they may not have explored on their own.

- o **Amper Music**, an AI-powered music composition platform, allows musicians and creators to generate original music tracks by selecting the mood, genre, and style. This is particularly useful for creating background music for videos, advertisements, or games without needing to compose music from scratch.

4. **AI in Fashion**:
   - o **The Fabricant**, a digital fashion house, specializes in AI-generated fashion pieces. They create **virtual-only collections** and showcase them in **digital fashion shows**. The AI generates fashion designs that are tailored to current trends, and the collection is sold as **digital garments** that users can wear in virtual environments, such as **avatars** in video games or on **social media platforms**.
   - o **Stitch Fix**, an AI-driven online styling service, uses generative AI to personalize fashion recommendations. By analyzing users' style preferences and data, Stitch Fix's AI suggests clothing items that are likely to fit their tastes, providing a highly customized shopping experience.

Summary

In this chapter, we explored the powerful **collaboration between humans and generative AI** in creative work. Rather than replacing human creativity, AI serves as a **co-creator, assistant**, and **augmenter**, enabling artists, writers, musicians, and designers to explore new ideas, generate variations, and refine their work more efficiently.

Generative AI tools are revolutionizing **art, writing**, and **music** by enabling creators to produce content more quickly, experiment with new concepts, and engage with their work in novel ways. Real-world examples, like AI-generated artwork, interactive storytelling, and AI-powered music platforms, highlight the vast potential of AI in creative industries.

The future of human-AI collaboration holds exciting possibilities, as generative AI continues to assist and inspire creative professionals in their work, leading to innovative and groundbreaking results across diverse fields.

CHAPTER TWENTYSEVEN

The Future of Generative AI

What's Next for Generative AI: Advanced Capabilities and Future Trends

The field of generative AI is rapidly evolving, with advancements happening at an unprecedented pace. As we look to the future, we can expect **more powerful models**, **advanced capabilities**, and **innovative applications** that push the boundaries of what AI can achieve. Here are some of the most exciting trends and developments on the horizon for generative AI:

1. **Larger, More Capable Models**:
   o As **computational power** continues to increase, we can expect the development of **larger, more sophisticated generative models**. These models will be able to process and generate more complex content across a wider range of domains, from text and images to audio and video. The size and complexity of models like **GPT-4**, **DALL·E 2**, and others are already showcasing the potential of large-scale AI, but future models will likely have even greater depth and versatility.
   o **Zero-shot learning**, where AI models can perform tasks without having been

explicitly trained on specific data for those tasks, will become more prevalent. This will allow AI to generalize across multiple domains, making it more adaptable and intelligent.

2. **Multimodal Generative Models**:
    o   We are moving towards **multimodal generative models** that can seamlessly integrate multiple types of data—text, images, audio, and video—into cohesive outputs. For instance, models that generate not just images from text prompts but entire **video narratives** or interactive simulations will become more common.
    o   These models will revolutionize industries such as **gaming**, **advertising**, and **virtual reality**, where the combination of text, visuals, and sounds is key to creating immersive and engaging experiences.

3. **Ethical and Responsible AI**:
    o   As generative AI becomes more powerful, **ethics** will continue to be a major area of focus. The potential for AI to generate **misleading** or **harmful content**, such as deepfakes or biased representations, will prompt further development of **safety measures** and **content moderation** tools. Researchers are working on ways to build models that are not only **more capable** but also **more responsible** and **accountable**.

- o We can expect significant improvements in AI's ability to detect and mitigate bias in generated content, ensuring that AI models reflect **fairness** and **diversity** in their outputs.
4. **Creativity at Scale**:
    - o The democratization of **AI-powered creativity** will continue to evolve, with more accessible tools enabling individuals and small businesses to generate high-quality creative content at scale. AI-powered platforms for art, music, design, and writing will enable anyone, regardless of their technical background, to create complex and personalized content.
    - o As AI models become increasingly adept at generating realistic and compelling creative work, we may see entirely **new forms of art** and **storytelling** emerge, blending traditional human creativity with machine-generated content in ways that were previously unimagined.

The Role of AI in Future Technologies: AGI, Robotics, and Autonomous Systems

The future of generative AI will be deeply intertwined with the development of **next-generation technologies**, including **Artificial General Intelligence (AGI)**, **robotics**, and **autonomous systems**. Here's how AI will shape these fields in the coming years:

1. **Artificial General Intelligence (AGI)**:
   - o **AGI** refers to AI that can perform any intellectual task that a human can do, possessing the ability to **understand, learn**, and **apply knowledge** across a wide variety of domains. While current AI models are narrow in their scope (specialized in a particular task), AGI represents a leap toward building machines with **broad cognitive capabilities**.
   - o As generative AI models evolve, they will move closer to the realization of AGI. In the future, **generative AI** will not only generate text, images, and videos but will be able to **solve problems, think critically**, and **reason across disciplines**—allowing AI to contribute in fields like **science, medicine**, and **policy-making**.

2. **AI in Robotics**:
   - o The integration of AI with **robotics** will enable machines to perform tasks in the physical world, from **manufacturing** and **logistics** to **healthcare** and **home assistance**. Generative AI will enhance robots' ability to adapt to complex environments and handle diverse tasks, such as **assembling objects, performing surgeries**, or **providing customer service**.
   - o AI-powered robots will also be able to generate new ways to approach physical

tasks by analyzing and optimizing their movements. For instance, robots in warehouses may use generative AI to **design optimal paths** for picking and storing goods, improving efficiency and reducing errors.

3. **Autonomous Systems**:
   - Generative AI will play a crucial role in the development of **autonomous systems**, such as **self-driving cars**, **drones**, and **autonomous ships**. These systems will use AI to navigate, make decisions, and generate responses to dynamic real-world situations.
   - For example, autonomous vehicles will leverage generative AI to generate simulations of different driving scenarios, helping improve safety features and decision-making processes in uncertain environments. AI will also generate models for predictive maintenance, helping ensure that autonomous systems function safely and efficiently.

4. **AI in Smart Environments**:
   - **Smart homes** and **smart cities** will rely on AI to optimize energy use, traffic flow, and public services. AI will generate data-driven solutions to improve urban planning, environmental sustainability, and public health.
   - In **smart homes**, AI-powered systems will generate personalized experiences for users, adjusting lighting, temperature,

and even entertainment options based on individual preferences and behaviors.

Final Thoughts: Preparing for a Future with AI-Driven Creativity

The future of generative AI is exciting, full of new possibilities for creative expression, technological advancement, and societal transformation. As AI continues to advance, it will play an increasingly central role in **shaping creativity**, **improving industries**, and **enhancing human experiences**. Here's how we can prepare for a future with AI-driven creativity:

1. **Embrace AI as a Tool, Not a Replacement**:
   o As we've seen throughout this book, AI should be viewed as a tool that enhances human capabilities rather than replacing them. Creative professionals can collaborate with AI to amplify their work, explore new ideas, and overcome creative blocks.
   o Embracing AI as a **co-creator** opens up new opportunities for artists, writers, musicians, designers, and innovators to push the boundaries of their fields, creating work that is richer, more diverse, and more personalized.
2. **Ethical AI Development**:
   o As generative AI becomes more pervasive, it's crucial that we focus on developing **ethical frameworks** that

guide its use. Ensuring that AI is transparent, fair, and accountable will be essential to prevent misuse and ensure that AI serves the greater good.

o Future AI systems should be designed with **responsibility** and **inclusivity** in mind, ensuring that they represent diverse perspectives and do not perpetuate harmful biases.

3. **Lifelong Learning and Adaptation**:

o As AI continues to evolve, individuals and organizations will need to continuously **adapt** and **learn** how to integrate AI tools into their workflows. **Lifelong learning** will become increasingly important as AI tools and capabilities evolve at a rapid pace.

o Whether it's learning how to use new generative AI models, understanding AI's ethical implications, or staying ahead of trends in creative fields, preparing for an AI-driven future will require **continuous engagement** with emerging technologies.

4. **AI and Human Creativity in Harmony**:

o The future will likely see a harmonious relationship between **human creativity** and **AI**. Instead of viewing AI as a threat, we should embrace it as a partner in the creative process, helping to create new forms of expression, new industries, and new ways of thinking.

o By combining the power of human imagination with the capabilities of AI, we can create a world where creativity knows no bounds, and technology serves as a force for good in shaping a more **inclusive, innovative,** and **dynamic** future.

Summary

In this chapter, we explored the **future of generative AI** and its potential to transform creative work, technology, and society. We discussed the exciting advancements ahead, including **larger, more capable models, multimodal AI**, and the evolution towards **AGI**. We also highlighted the critical role that AI will play in fields such as **robotics, autonomous systems,** and **smart environments**.

As we prepare for a future with AI-driven creativity, it's important to view AI as a **tool** that enhances human potential, fosters collaboration, and opens up new possibilities for innovation. By focusing on **ethical AI development, lifelong learning,** and **creative partnerships** with AI, we can ensure that AI will serve as a powerful ally in shaping a brighter, more creative future for all.

www.ingramcontent.com/pod-product-compliance
Lightning Source LLC
LaVergne TN
LVHW022339060326
832902LV00022B/4141

* 9 7 9 8 3 0 8 5 8 7 5 1 4 *